Anonymous

Our Cooks in Council

A Manual of Practical and Economical Recipes for the Household

Anonymous

Our Cooks in Council
A Manual of Practical and Economical Recipes for the Household

ISBN/EAN: 9783744792554

Printed in Europe, USA, Canada, Australia, Japan

Cover: Foto ©Andreas Hilbeck / pixelio.de

More available books at **www.hansebooks.com**

A MANUAL

OF

Practical and Economical Recipes

FOR THE HOUSEHOLD.

Published by the
LADIES OF THE CONGREGATIONAL CHURCH
OF JEFFERSON, O.

1881.

TABLE OF CONTENTS.

	PAGE.
Introduction	5
Soups	7
Shell Fish	12
Fish	17
Poultry	21
Meats	26
Relish for Meats	37
Salads	38
Game	40
Vegetables	42
Eggs	48
Bread	50
Breakfast Cakes	56
Crackers	58
Cakes	59
Icing for Cake	76
Cookies	77
Ginger Cookies	79
Ginger Bread	81
Doughnuts	83
Crullers	85
Pies	86
Puddings	92
Pudding Sauce	101
Ambrosia, Custards, &c.	103
Pickles	109
Fruit, Jellies, Preserves, &c.	117
Confectionery	124
Drinks	126
The Sick Room	127
Miscellaneous	136
Index	154

INTRODUCTION.

This little volume is sent out by the ladies of the Congregational Church of Jefferson to take a place among the many cook books already extant, in the hope—common with them—of promoting healthful and economical cooking.

They are frank to say, also, with this laudable purpose they hope to aid an enterprise connected with their church.

The recipes have been furnished by practical, successful housekeepers, and will be found reliable in every case.

The laborer and the professional man needs plain, nutritious food properly prepared, nor should the polite dinner transgress a single law of health.

Napoleon said, "An army moves upon its stomach;" and a certain divine affirms that much religious despondency is due to indigestion. Since health and happiness so largely depend on palatable and wholesome food, the best system of cooking should be followed.

We often hear such remarks as: "I had poor *luck* with my bread today." "I didn't *hit it right* on my cake," while the truth is, such cooking is done in ignorance or inexcusable carelessness.

Cooking is an art; and to be a success it is necessary first to have a good *rule*, and then carefully follow it. Sound judgment must be exercised it is true, and caution in regulating the fire, but people who have no "knack," as they say, can cook well if they follow good recipes, and further, it is their duty.

Mrs. Carlyle spent the first month of her married life crying over repeated failures, but through studious persistence she became accomplished in household duties, and this may have been one reason why her husband, great philosopher as he was, thought her the most remarkable woman, and best wife in the world.

In the Miscellaneous department will be found important suggestions upon a variety of subjects needed every day in every household. An index is appended.

That many may find the work helpful in their daily tasks is the wish of the

COOKS IN COUNCIL.

OUR COOKS IN COUNCIL.

SOUPS.

To prepare good stock the meat should be fresh, lean and juicy to make the best soup. If it is to be eaten as soon as it is prepared, you should remove all the fat possible from the meat, for there is nothing more disagreeable than very greasy soup. If it is to be eaten next day, or later, stand the stock in a cool place, and remove all the grease from the top the next morning.

Beef alone, with some vegetables, will make a good stock, but many people think that by adding chicken or veal it makes a soup of finer flavor; others think the addition of a ham bone a great improvement to the broth or stock. Stock can be made from the trimmings of fresh meat, or from the bones of any meat or fowl.

Having selected your meat, put it into cold water, about three pints to every pound of meat, and let it simmer slowly from one side, taking pains to remove all scum that rises. Should always keep your kettle covered, so as to retain all the flavor possible. Put in but little salt at first, and add salt, pepper, etc., to suit the taste when nearly done. It usually takes from three to five hours to cook the meat properly and make good broth or stock. When it has cooked say three hours, and all the scum has been removed, add one or two onions, fried brown in butter, and one or two carrots, or any other vegetable that you may prefer, but do not put in any vegetables till all the scum has been removed. If more water is needed, always add boiling water.

Stock that is to be kept should always be strained into an earthen jar as soon as it is done, for it injures the color and flavor to stand in an iron pot. Stock should be kept in a cool place. It will form a jelly, and keep for a week or longer.

By adding macaroni, vermicelli, etc., to stock, you can have almost any soup you may desire. It also makes very fine gravy by cutting off a piece of stock jelly and heating, thickening, and seasoning to taste.

Savory herbs should always be at hand, for they are almost indispensable to good cooking. The relish of a dish depends very much upon its savor, or taste, which can be changed almost as much as you please by using different savory herbs. Summer savory, sage, thyme, sweet marjoram, sweet basil, rosemary, bay leaves, and fennel, are among the best of the savory herbs. They can be purchased at almost any drug store and cost but little; but many people prefer to raise most of their savory herbs, which can be done with but little trouble.

Browning for Soups.

Many of the nicest soups owe their attractive appearance to burnt sugar, which is prepared as follows: Put three tablespoonfuls of brown sugar and an ounce of butter in a small frying-pan and set it over the fire; stir continually until it is of a bright brown color, add half a pint of water, boil and skim, and when cold bottle for use. Add to soups at discretion just before serving.

Bean Soup.

Soak one and a half pints of beans in cold water over night. In the morning drain off the water, wash the beans in fresh water and put into soup kettle, with four quarts of good beef stock, from which all the fat has been removed. Set it where it will boil slowly but steadily till dinner, or three hours at the least. Two hours before dinner slice in an onion and a carrot. Some think it improved by adding a little tomato. If the beans are not liked whole, strain through a colander and send to the table hot.

Beef Soup.

Boil a soup bone about four hours, then take out meat into a chopping-bowl; put the bones back into the kettle. Slice very thin one small onion, six potatoes and three turnips into the soup. Boil until all are tender. Have at least one gallon of soup when done. It is improved by adding crackers rolled, or noodles, just before taking off. Take the meat that has been cut from the bones, chop fine while warm, season with salt and pepper, add one teacup of soup saved out before putting in the vegetables. Pack in a dish, and slice down for tea or lunch when cold.

Celery Soup.

One shank of beef, one large bunch of celery, one cup of rich cream. Make a good broth of a shank of beef, skim off the fat and thicken the broth with a little flour mixed with water. Cut into small pieces one large bunch of celery, or two small ones, boiling them in the soup till tender. Add a cup of rich cream with pepper and salt.

Chicken Soup.

Boil a pair of chickens with great care, skimming constantly and keeping them covered with water. When tender, take out the chicken and remove the bone. Put a large lump of butter into a spider, dredge the chicken-meat well with flour, and lay in the hot pan; fry a nice brown, and keep hot and dry. Take a pint of the chicken water, and stir in two large spoonfuls of curry powder, two of butter and one of flour, one teaspoonful of salt and a little cayenne; stir until smooth, then mix it with the broth in the pot. When well mixed, simmer five minutes, then add the browned chicken. Serve with rice.

French Vegetable Soup.

To a leg of lamb of moderate size take four quarts of water. Of carrots, potatoes, onions, tomatoes, cabbage, and turnips, take a teacup each, chopped fine; salt and pepper to taste. Let the lamb be boiled in this water. Let it cool; skim off all the fat that rises to the top. The next day boil again, adding the chopped vegetables. Let it boil three hours the second day.

Fish Chowder.

. Take a fresh haddock, of three or four pounds, clean it well, and cut in pieces of three inches square. Place in the bottom of your dinner-pot five or six slices of salt pork; fry brown, then add three onions sliced thin, and fry those brown. Remove the kettle from the fire, and place on the onions and pork a layer of fish; sprinkle over a little pepper and salt, then a layer of pared and sliced potatoes, a layer of fish and potatoes, till the fish is used up. Cover with water, and let it boil for half an hour. Pound six biscuits or crackers as fine as meal, and pour into the pot; and, lastly, add a quart or pint of milk; let it scald well and serve.

Fish Chowder.

Take a pound of salt pork, cut into strips, and soak in hot water for five minutes. Cover the bottom of a pot with a layer of this. Cut four pounds of cod or sea-bass into pieces two inches square, and lay enough of these on the pork to cover it. Follow with a layer of chopped onions, a little parsley, summer savory and pepper, either black or cayenne. Then a layer of split Boston or butter or whole cream crackers, which have been soaked in warm water until moist through, but not ready to break. Above this lay a stratum of pork, and repeat the order given above— onions, seasoning (not too much), crackers and pork, until your materials are exhausted. Let the topmost layer be buttered crackers well soaked. Pour in enough cold water to cover all barely. Cover the pot, stew gently for an hour, watching that the water does not sink too low. Should it leave the upper layer exposed, replenish cautiously from the boiling tea-kttle. When the chowder is thoroughly done, take out with a perforated skimmer and put into a tureen. Thicken the gravy with a tablespoon of flour and about the same quantity of butter. Boil up and pour over the chowder. Send sliced lemon, pickles and stewed tomatoes to the table with it, that the guests may add, if they like.

Stock for Soup.

Have a large pot on the back of the stove. Put in lean beef, either after having been cooked or before, in the proportion of one pound of beef to one quart of water. Add pork rinds with all the fat taken off. This may cook slowly two or three days. When cold, skim off all the fat and put into another vessel. This stock may be used for all soups in which meat-broth is required. By adding for thickening either barley, rice, sago, macaroni or vermicelli, it will make any of these soups.

Tomato Soup.
Mrs. W. P. Howland.

To one quart of water add eight large tomatoes; cut in pieces and boil twenty minutes, add one-half teaspoon of soda and boil a few minutes more, then add a pint of sweet milk, then season as you would oysters. Bread crumbs, sago, barley or rice may be added.

Noodles for Soup.

Beat one egg light; add a pinch of salt and flour enough to make a stiff dough; roll out in a very thin sheet, dredge with flour to keep from sticking, then roll up tightly. Begin at one end and shave down fine, like cabbage for slaw.

Harvest Soup.

Cut in small pieces one pound of good beef, cover with cold water, and boil gently for three hours; let it stand over night; remove all the fat; bring to a boil and add one can of lobster cut fine; prepare one cauliflower sliced, cut the corn from one dozen ears, break in small pieces one quart of butter beans, slice one onion, cut fine three or four radishes, and add all to the soup, with one whole green bull-pepper, one-half teaspoonful black pepper, one teaspoonful salt. In one hour add one quart of tomatoes sliced. When tender, carefully remove, without breaking, on a skimmer the bull-pepper; simmer the rest four hours longer; add no more water before the tomatoes are put in than necessary to keep from burning; after they are in none will be needed. Half the above quantities can be used. Some like potato with the other vegetables. Add salt to taste before dishing. A little rice can be used if liked in the soup.

SHELL FISH.

Lobster Croquettes.

Chop the lobster very fine; mix with pepper, salt, bread crumbs and a little parsley; moisten with cream and a small piece of butter; shape with your hands; dip in egg, roll in bread crumbs, and fry.

Lobster Cutlets.

Mince the flesh of lobters fine; season with salt, pepper and spice; melt a piece of butter in a saucepan; mix with it one tablespoonful of flour; add lobster, finely-chopped parsley, mix with some good stock; remove from the fire, and stir into it the yolks of two eggs; spread out the mixture, and, when cold, cut into cutlets, dip carefully into beaten egg, then into fine baked bread crumbs; let them stand an hour, and repeat, and fry a rich brown. Serve with fried parsley.

Lobster Rissoles.

Boil the lobster, take out the meat, mince it fine, pound the coral smooth, and grate for one lobster the yolks of three hard-boiled eggs; season with cayenne and a little salt: make a batter of milk, flour and well-beaten eggs—two tablespoonfuls of milk and one of flour to each egg; beat the batter well; mix the lobster with it gradually until stiff enough to roll into balls the size of a walnut; fry in fresh butter, or best salad oil, and serve.

Broiled Oysters.

Drain select oysters in a colander. Dip them one by one into melted butter, to prevent sticking to the gridiron, and place them on a wire gridiron. Broil over a clear fire. When nicely browned on both sides, season with salt, pepper, and plenty of butter, and lay them on hot buttered toast, moistened with a little hot water. Serve very hot, or they will not be nice. Oysters cooked in this way and served on broiled beefsteak are nice.

Fried Oysters.
Mrs. S. A. Northway.

When the oysters are taken from the pan, wrap them in a dry cloth until the surface moisture of the oyster is absorbed: then dip them in the white of an egg slightly beaten, from that into pulverized cracker, allowing all that will to adhere to the oyster; then heat together as hot as possible, equal parts of butter and lard, in which fry them quickly.

Fried Oysters.
Mrs. B. W. Baldwin.

Wipe the oysters on a napkin. Then dip them in well-beaten egg—then in Indian meal, or rolled cracker, or best of all is bread dried in the oven until a light brown and ground in the coffee mill. Fry in butter. Salt while frying.

Oyster Pie.

Make a rich puff paste; roll out twice as thick as for a fruit pie, for the top crust—about the ordinary thickness for the lower. Line a pudding dish with the thinner, and fill with crusts of dry bread or light crackers. Some use a folded towel to fill the interior of the pie, but the above expedient is preferable. Butter the edges of the dish, that you may be able to lift the upper crust without breaking. Cover the mock pie with the thick crust, ornamented heavily at the edge, that it may lie more quietly, and bake. Cook the oysters as for a stew, only beating into them at the last, two eggs, and thickening with a spoonful of fine cracker crumbs or rice flour. They should stew but five minutes, and time them so that the paste will be baked just in season to receive them. Lift the top crust, pour in the smoking hot oysters, and send up hot.

Many consider it unnecessary to prepare the oysters and crust separately; but experience and observation go to prove that if the precaution be omitted, the oysters are apt to be woefully overdone. The maker can try both methods and take her choice.

Pickled Oysters.
Mrs. E. H. Way.

Take one hundred large fine oysters and pick off carefully the bits of shell that may be hanging to them. Lay the oysters in a deep dish and then strain the liquor over them. Put them in an iron skillet that is lined with porcelain, and add salt to your taste. Without salt they will not be firm enough. Set the skillet upon hot coals, and allow the oysters to simmer till they are heated through, but not until they boil. Then take out the oysters and put them into a stone jar, leaving the liquor in the skillet.

Add to it a pint of clear cider vinegar, a large teaspoonful of blades of mace, three dozen whole cloves and three dozen whole pepper corns. Let it come to a boil, and when the oysters are quite cold in the jar, pour the liquor on them. The spices may be changed if desired. They are fit for use immediately, but are better the next day. In cold weather they will keep a week.

If you intend sending them a considerable distance, you must allow the oysters to boil, and double the proportions of the pickle and spices.

Oysters with Toast.

Broil or fry as many oysters as you wish, and lay them on buttered toast; salt and pepper; pour over them a cup of hot, rich cream; keep them perfectly hot until eaten.

Roasted Oysters.

Take oysters in the shell, wash the shells clean, and lay them on hot coals; when they are done they will begin to open. Remove the upper shell, and serve the oysters in the lower shell, with a little melted butter poured over each.

Oysters, Fancy Roast.

Toast a few slices of bread, and butter them; lay them in a shallow dish; put on the liquor of the oysters to heat; add salt and pepper, and just before it boils add the oysters; let them boil up once, and pour over the bread.

Stewed Oysters.

Take one quart of liquor oysters; put the liquor (a teacupful for three) in a stew pan, and add half as much more water, salt, a good bit of pepper, a teaspoonful of rolled crackers for each. Put on the stove and let it boil. Have your oysters ready in a bowl, and the moment the liquor boils, pour in all your oysters, say ten for each person, or six will do. Now watch carefully, and as soon as it begins to boil take out your watch, count just thirty seconds, and take your oysters from the stove. You will have your big dish ready, with one and a half tablespoonfuls of cream or milk for each person. Pour your stew on this, and serve immediately. Never boil an oyster in milk, if you wish it to be good.

Maryland Stewed Oysters.

Put the juice into a saucepan and let it simmer, skimming it carefully; then rub the yolks of three hard-boiled eggs and a large spoonful of flour well together, and stir into the juice. Cut in small pieces a quarter of a pound of butter, half a teaspoonful of whole allspice, a little salt, a little cayenne, and the juice of a fresh lemon; let all simmer ten minutes, and just before dishing add the oysters. This is for two quarts of oysters.

Yacht Oyster Stew.

Strain, cook, and skim the juice of twenty-four oysters; boil celery and quarter of a small onion in a little water for half an hour, or until the celery is well cooked; then add a pint of milk or cream, a tablespoon of butter, a tablespoon of pounded crackers, a teaspoon of Worcestershire sauce, salt, pepper the oysters and cooked juice. and boil all three minutes, or until the edges of the oysters shrivel.

Oyster Fritters.

One hundred oysters, six eggs, two cupfuls cracker-dust, half cupful wheat flour, milk enough to make a thick batter; drain the oysters through a colander; beat the whites and yolks of the eggs separately; two teaspoonfuls of baking powder put in last; little dust of pepper.—L. I. C.

Panned Oysters.
Mrs. S. A. Northway.

Drain the oysters very dry, place the drippings in a porcelain kettle, add one-half cup boiling water, season highly with butter, pepper and salt; cream the butter with a little corn-starch, just enough to make the liquid creamy. After this boils add one-half quart of rich sweet cream; pour the oysters into a scalding hot spider and turn them over and over until they are scalded through; bake some crackers, place them in a deep dish which has been previously heated, then put in the oysters, and lastly the boiling hot sauce. Serve in small dishes, nice for a breakfast or tea party.

Scalloped Oysters.
Mrs. B. W. Baldwin.

To one can of oysters allow one teacupful of broken (not rolled) crackers, one-half cup of milk, one and one-half cups of oyster liquor and water, not quite one-half pound of butter. Place a layer of oysters in the bottom of pan, then layer of crackers; sprinkle plentifully with salt, pepper and bits of butter, then another layer of oysters, salt, pepper and butter; beat one egg, add to it the milk and water, and pour carefully over the whole; cover and place in hot oven; when steamed through remove the cover and brown slightly. Never have more than two layers each to a pan. Eight cans will feed fifty-five persons.

Oyster Soup with Milk.
Mrs. E. F. Mason.

Pour one quart of cold water over one quart of oysters; drain through a colander, boil and skim; add the oysters and one-half cup of rolled crackers; season with pepper, and salt, and then add one quart of new milk, brought to boiling point in a pail set in boiling water. Serve at once.

Plain Oyster Soup.

Pour one quart of oysters in colander; rinse by pouring over them one pint of cold water; add one pint of boiling water; let boil; skim; season with pepper, butter (size of an egg); then add oysters; let boil up once only; season with salt and serve.

Clam Chowder.

Fry five or six slices of fat pork, crisp, and chop to pieces. Sprinkle some of these in the bottom of a pot; lay upon them a stratum of clams; sprinkle with cayenne or black pepper and salt, and scatter bits of butter profusely over all; next, have a layer of chopped onions, then one of small crackers split and moistened with warm milk. On these pour a little of the fat left in the pan after the pork is fried, and then comes a new round of pork, clams, onions, etc. Proceed in this order until the pot is nearly full, then cover with water, and stew slowly—the pot closely covered—for three-quarters of an hour. Drain off all the liquor that will flow freely, and when you have turned the chowder into the tureen, return the gravy to the pot. Thicken with flour, or, better still, pounded crackers; add a glass of wine, some catsup and spiced sauce; boil it up and pour it over the contents of the tureen. Send around walnut or butternut pickles with it.

Clam Stew.

To one-half peck of hard-shell clams add one teacup of water, and steam until shells open; take out of shells, then strain the juice, add it to the clams, and when they come to a boil add one pint of milk, piece of butter (size of an egg), three rolled crackers, pepper and salt if needed.

FISH.

Fish when fresh are hard when pressed by the finger—the gills red—the eyes full. If the flesh is flabby and the eyes sunken, the fish are stale. They should be thoroughly cleaned, washed, and sprinkled with salt.

Before broiling fish, rub the gridiron with a piece of fat, to prevent its sticking. Lay the skin side down first.

The earthy taste often found in fresh water fish can be removed by soaking in salt and water.

Most kinds of salt fish should be soaked in cold water for twenty-four hours—the fleshy side turned down in the water.

Fish may be scaled much easier by dipping into boiling water about a minute.

Fish may as well be scaled, if desired, before packing down in salt, though in that case do not scald them.

Salt fish are quickest and best freshened by soaking in sour milk.

How to Cook Codfish.
Mrs. H. L. Hervey.

Soak the thickest part for two days in sweet skimmed milk. Roll in flour and fry quite brown. Scald, but do not boil, one teacup of sweet cream, and pour over the fish.

Another Way.

Remove the skin and bone. Make the fish fine by cutting it first in short pieces, then pick very fine; throw into cold water for ten or fifteen minutes; keep in a warm place. Then pour off the water, add a cup of milk and piece of butter, size of an egg; cook slowly fifteen minutes, then mix together one tablespoon of flour and one-half cup of sweet cream, and pour in the fish, letting it boil just a moment, when it will be ready for the table.

Codfish on Toast.

Take a bowl full of shredded codfish, put this in cold water in a skillet. Let it come to a boil, then turn into a colander to drain. Turn into the skillet again with a little cold milk; season with butter and pepper; stir smooth a tablespoonful of flour with a little cold milk; add, and let it boil for a moment; turn this on to buttered toast on a platter.

Fish Fritters.

Take salt codfish, soak it over night. In the morning throw the water off the fish, put on fresh and set it on the range until it comes to a boil. Do not let it boil, as that will harden it. Then pick it up very fine, season with pepper, mace, and perhaps a little salt. Make a batter of a pint of milk and three eggs, stir in the fish and fry in small cakes. Any kind of cold fish makes nice fritters.

Fish Cakes.

One pint bowl of salt codfish, picked very fine, two pint bowls of whole, raw, peeled potatoes; put together in cold water and boil till the potatoes are thoroughly cooked; remove from fire and drain off all the water, mash with potato masher, add piece of butter, the size of an egg, two well beaten eggs and a little pepper; mix well with a wooden spoon; have a frying pan with boiling lard or drippings, into which drop a spoonful of mixture, and fry brown; do not freshen the fish before boiling with potatoes, and do not mold cakes, but drop from spoon.

Codfish Balls.
Mrs. S. A. Northway.

Pick the fish into small pieces; soak in plenty of water until fresh enough for the table; then chop very fine a little fried pork, put it and the fat fried out of it with the fish; stir in one or more beaten eggs, according to the quantity of fish; add as much mashed and seasoned potato as there is the fish; make into balls, roll in flour, drop them into fat, the same as doughnuts.

Baked Fish.
Mrs. B. C. Bowman, Jr.

One good sized fish (fresh); make a stuffing same as for chicken. Fill the fish, and bind thin slices of salt pork around the fish, and bake same as you would chicken.

Baked White Fish.
Mrs. E. J. Betts.

Freshen the fish; put it in as small a pan as possible, and bake five minutes; then pour off the liquid; pour over it one-half pint cream, in which two tablespoons of flour have been stirred; sprinkle with pepper, bake until brown.

Baked Shad.

Make a stuffing of grated bread-crumbs, cold ham, or bacon, minced fine, a little sweet marjoram, cayenne pepper, a pinch of mace, and as much cloves as you can take up on the point of a pen-knife; moisten with yolk of egg; fill the inside of the fish, and put a little of the stuffing over the outside; place in a baking-pan, a very little water, some butter and flour rubbed to a cream, a gill of port wine, and the juice of a lemon; garnish with sliced lemon, very thin.

Baked Fresh Fish.

Open the fish so that it will lay perfectly flat. Rub salt over it, and lay it in a dripping pan with a very little butter and water. Put it in a very hot oven and bake twenty minutes or a half hour, according to the thickness of the fish.

When done it will be a delicate brown, and will be cooked through without the trouble of turning. Of course the skin side is laid next to the pan.

White fish cooked in this way are especially nice.

Flaked Fish.

Make a sauce by dredging some flour into two ounces of hot water in a stew-pan; add half a pound of cold fish, nicely flaked, one ounce of cold butter, a dessert-spoonful each of anchovy sauce and mixed mustard, one teacupful of cream, some pepper, salt, and a few bread crumbs. Make hot and serve as it is, or you may pour it into a buttered dish, with the addition of a few bread crumbs, and brown the top in the oven.

Pickled Salmon.

Soak salt salmon twenty-four hours, changing the water frequently; afterwards pour boiling water AROUND it, and let it stand fifteen minutes; drain off and then pour on boiling vinegar with cloves and mace added.

Boiled Salt Mackerel.

After freshening fold in a cloth and simmer 15 minutes, when water reaches boiling point it is nearly done; remove, pour over it drawn butter with two sliced hard-boiled eggs, and trim with parsley leaves. Boiling salt fish hardens it.

Boiled Fresh Mackerel.

Wash the mackerel with a cloth dipped in vinegar, then wrap and sew a cloth well floured around it and boil ½ hour. Serve with sauce made of part of the water in which it was boiled, seasoned with butter, pepper and salt, juice of half a lemon, or any other sauce with catsup as preferred.

Fish Pie.

Take any of the firm-fleshed fish, cut in slices, and season with salt and pepper; let them stand in a very cool place for two or three hours, then put them in a baking dish, with a little cream or water and butter and flour rubbed to a cream, with minced parsley and hard boiled eggs sliced; line the sides of the dish half-way down, and cover with a nice paste. Bake in an oven, quick at first, but gradually growing moderate.

Fish Salad.

Pick up cold fish and place in a frying-pan; season with salt and pepper; the juice of a lemon and melted butter, a little vinegar, and one raw egg beaten; let warm over a slow fire, stirring so that they do not burn; place in a dish; serve cold.

POULTRY.

How to Choose Poultry.

Young, plump, and well-fed, but not too fat poultry are the best. The skin should be fine grained, clear and white; the breast full, fleshed, and broad; the legs smooth. The birds must be heavy in proportion to their size. As regards ducks and geese, their breasts must also be plump; the feet flexible and yellow. For boiling, white-legged poultry must be chosen, because when dressed their appearance is by far the more delicate. But dark-legged ones are juicy and of a better flavor when roasted. The greatest precaution ought to be taken to prevent poultry from getting at all tainted before it is cooked. It should be killed and dressed from eight to ten hours before cooking. Pigeons are far better for being cooked the day they are killed, as they lose their flavor by hanging. Care must be taken to cook poultry thoroughly, for nothing is more revolting to the palate than underdone poultry.

Chicken Pot-Pie.

Cut and joint the chicken, cover with water, and let it boil gently until tender. Season with salt and pepper, and thicken the gravy with two tablespoonfuls of flour mixed smooth in a piece of butter the size of an egg. Have ready nice light bread dough; cut with a biscuit-cutter about an inch thick; drop this into the boiling gravy, having previously removed the chicken to a hot platter; cover, and let it boil from half to three-quarters of an hour. To ascertain whether they are done or not, stick into one of them a fork, and if it comes out clean, they are done. Lay on the platter with the chicken, pour over the gravy and serve.

Fried Chicken.

Joint young, tender chickens; if old, put in a stew-pan with a little water, and simmer gently till tender; season with salt and pepper, dip into flour, and fry in hot lard and butter until nicely browned. Lay on a hot platter and take the liquor in which the chicken was stewed, turn into the frying-pan with the browned gravy, stir in a little flour; when it has boiled, stir in a teacup of rich, sweet cream, and pour over the chicken.

Turkey Scallop.

Pick the meat from the bones of cold turkey, and chop it fine. Put a layer of bread-crumbs on the bottom of a buttered dish, moisten them with a little milk, then put in a layer of turkey with some of the filling, and cut small pieces of butter over the top; sprinkle with pepper and salt; then another layer of bread crumbs, and so on until the dish is nearly full; add a little hot water to the gravy left from the turkey, and pour over it. Then take two eggs, two tablespoonfuls of milk, one of melted butter, a little salt, and cracker crumbs as much as will make it thick enough to spread on with a knife, put bits of butter over it, and cover with a plate. Bake three-quarters of an hour. About ten minutes before serving, remove the plate and let it brown.

Scalloped Chicken.

Mince cold chicken and a little lean ham quite fine, season with pepper and a little salt; stir all together, add some sweet cream, enough to make it quite moist, cover with crumbs, put it into scallop shells or a flat dish, put a little butter on top, and brown before the fire or front of a range.

Chestnut Stuffing.

Boil the chestnuts and shell them, then blanch them and boil until soft: mash them fine and mix with a little sweet cream, some bread crumbs, pepper and salt. For turkey.

A good way to cook Chickens.

Take three or four chickens, and, after cleaning and washing them well in cold water, split them down the back, break the breast bone and unjoint the wings to make them lie down better; put them in a large bread-pan and sprinkle pepper, salt, and flour over them, put a large lump of fresh butter on each chicken, pour boiling water in the pan and set in the oven. Let them cook till very tender and a rich brown color; then take out on a large platter, put on more butter, and set in the oven to keep warm; put some sweet cream in the pan and add as much hot water as you think necessary for the quantity of gravy you desire, though the more cream and the less water, the better the gravy. Thicken with flour; put a pint of the gravy on the chickens. They must be put on the table very hot.

Red Brook Mushroom Chicken Fry.
J. A. Howells.

Put on the chicken and par-boil until quite tender. Pick over fresh mushrooms and rinse in clear cold water, enough if you have them, to cover the chicken, in a deep spider or shallow stew-pan. Put in a lump of butter, salt and pepper to suit taste. Fry down brown and serve hot.

NOTE.—If there are more than two persons to sit down to this dish, it will be well to have more than one chicken.

Chicken Pie.

Stew chicken till tender, season with one-quarter lb. butter, salt and pepper; line the sides of a pudding-dish with a rich crust, pour in the stewed chicken and cover closely with a crust, first cutting a hole in the centre. Have ready a can of oysters; heat the liquor, thicken with a little flour and water, and season with salt, pepper, and butter. When it comes to a boil, pour over the oysters, and, about twenty minutes before the pie is done, lift the top crust and put them in.

Crust for Chicken Pie.

1 pint buttermilk; 1 cup shortening, 1 teaspoonful of soda.

Stewed Chicken with Oysters.

Season and stew a chicken in a quart of water until very tender; take it out on a hot dish and keep it warm; then put into the liquor a lump of butter the size of an egg: mix a little flour and water smooth and make thick gravy; season well with pepper and salt and let it come to a boil. Have ready a quart of oysters picked over, and put them in without any liquor. Stir them round, and as soon as they are cooked, pour all over the chicken.

Roast Turkey.
Mrs. E. F. Mason.

In drawing, leave all the fat in the fowl, wash and rinse well, drying inside and out with a towel. For the stuffing of a turkey weighing from 20 to 25 pounds, allow from 75 to 100 oysters with their liquor, one-half lb. butter, pepper, salt and sage to taste, with enough bread to mix with the other ingredients, two eggs. Boil the oyster liquor and strain it over the bread, add the seasoning, and if more moisture is needed, add boiling water. When this is cool, put in the oysters, taking care not to break them. If oysters are not used, chop the giblets with the stuffing. Unless the turkey is to be roasted the day it is stuffed, the dressing should be entirely cold. Baste turkey frequently while baking.

Baked Chicken.
Mrs. E. H. Way.

Cut the chicken into small pieces, and remove all the skin; put it into a kettle with water enough to boil, to which add a little salt. When the chicken is almost done take it out of the kettle, roll each piece in flour, sprinkle with pepper and salt, lay it in a dripping-pan, put a small piece of butter on each piece, and add sufficient boiling water to baste with. When brown make a gravy of the liquor the chicken was boiled in, with a little flour and an egg (if desired) well beaten; pour it over the chicken and return to the oven for a few minutes, then serve.

Chicken Loaf.
Mrs. Chamberlain, Geneva O.

Take two large full-grown chickens; cook as usual (salt pork in slices cooked with them improves the flavor); season with pepper, salt and sage; when tender, chop all the meat, then add grated bread, one-half the bulk of chicken, pour in the thickened gravy, add three well-beaten eggs; bake one hour in moderate oven; press with heavy weights while cooling; when cold slice. Very nice for lunch, and is sufficient for thirty persons.

Pressed Chicken.
Miss Fanny Dean.

Boil the chicken until tender; if there is more than one-half pint to a chicken, boil it down; remove the meat from the bones; keep the light and dark separate; chop with two small slices of bread to each chicken; season with butter, salt and pepper; add the soup, take a narrow bread tin, place first the dark and then the light meat, press solid; put in a cool place. When cold, warm the pan and turn it out on a meat board; it will slice nicely. Other meat can be pressed in the same way.

Macaroni Timbles.
Mrs. McCall.

The breast of four pounds chicken, whites of three eggs, one tablespoon melted butter, three tablespoons thick cream (or milk can be used), four tablespoons of the juice of the chicken; the chicken should be boiled tender in as little water as necessary to cook it in; pepper and salt to taste, with a very little nutmeg; chop all fine and pass it through a sieve, then beat light with a spoon; add a few drops of lemon juice; take one-fourth pound of macaroni boiled not very soft, throw it into cold water, then cut it in pieces about one-fourth inch long, butter the cups, and stick the macaroni around and around to the edge of the cup; then pour in the mixture about two-thirds full; put a buttered paper over the top of each cup, and steam one-half hour; turn out when done on to a suitable dish, and pour over a drawn butter sauce, about as thick as rich cream. One tablespoon of sherry wine improves the sauce. The timbles, when well made, resemble little bee hives with honey cells, and are a pretty dish on a dinner table.

Baked Chicken.
Mrs. J. E. Allen.

Take a young chicken, cut it up as for boiling, lay in a dripping pan and sprinkle with salt; spread over it a dressing, made by stirring butter and flour together until stiff enough to spread easily; pour over it two-thirds teacup of water, and bake. It will cook nearly as quickly as potatoes. When done, take out and pour in hot water, and stir until the dressing is thin enough.

MEATS.

In selecting beef, choose that of a fine, smooth grain, of a bright red color and white fat.

The sixth, seventh, and eighth ribs are the choicest cuts for a roast. Have the bones removed and the meat rolled, but have the butcher send the bones for soup.

The flesh of good veal is firm and dry, and the joints stiff.

The flesh of good mutton, or lamb, is a bright red, with the fat firm and white.

If the meat of pork is young, the lean will break on being pinched. The fat will be white, soft and pulpy.

Rules for Boiling Meat.

All fresh meat should be put to cook in boiling water; then the outer part contracts, and the internal juices are preserved. For making soup, put on in cold water. All salt meat should be put on in cold water, that the salt may be extracted in cooking. In boiling meats, it is important to keep the water constantly boiling, otherwise the meat will absorb the water. Be careful to add boiling water, if more is needed. Remove the scum when it first begins to boil. Allow about twenty minutes for boiling for each pound of fresh meat. The more gently meat boils the more tender it will be.

To broil meat well, have your gridiron hot before you put the meat on.

Broil steak without salting.

In roasting beef, it is necessary to have a brisk fire. Baste often. Season when nearly done.

To prevent meat from scorching during roasting, place a basin of water in the oven; the steam generated prevents scorching, and makes the meat cook better.

Frying Meats.

Frying is often a convenient mode of cookery. It may be performed by a fire which will not do for roasting or boiling. For general purposes, and especially for fish, pork fat is preferable to lard. To know when the fat is of a proper heat—according to what you are to fry—is the real great secret of frying.

To fry fish, potatoes, or anything that is watery, the fire

must be very clear, and the fat quite hot; which you may be perfectly sure of when it has done hissing, and is still. If the fat is not very hot, you cannot fry fish, either to a good color, or firm and crisp.

Beefsteak—Scalloped.
Mrs. B. W. Baldwin.

Chop very fine raw steak; butter a tin; place in it a layer of the chopped meat; then a layer of bread-crumbs; on this bits of butter, pepper and salt; then another layer of meat and bread, pepper and salt; beat one egg thoroughly, add one-half teacupful of milk and one-half cupful of water; pour carefully over the top; stick bits of butter thickly over the top; bake one-half to three-quarters of an hour. Cover the dish until steamed through, then remove and brown.

Broiled Steak.
Mrs. B. F. Bowman, Jr.

Grease the gridiron or broiler with pork or suet; have it hot; put on the steak over hot coals; cover. In a moment, when the steak is colored, turn it over. Watch and turn frequently. Do not let out the juice by sticking the fork in it; remove to a hot ptlater; sprinkle well with salt and pepper, and butter well; set platter in the oven a few moments to let butter soak in well. The juice of a good steak is inside, not in the gravy dish.

Baked Steak.
Mrs. S. A. Northway.

Take a tender round-steak, cut thick, rub on salt and pepper, prepare stale bread like stuffing for turkey, spread over the steak, roll tightly, and fasten with skewers; bake until tender. This is very nice sliced, and eaten cold.

Mushrooms with Steak.
Mrs. J. A. Howells.

Cook steak in ordinary way; cover top of steak thickly with mushrooms; season with pepper, butter and salt to taste; cover closely, and steam ten minutes, stirring occasionally.

Beefsteak and Onions.

Prepare the steak as usual; while it is broiling put three or four chopped onions in a frying-pan with a little beef dripping or butter; stir and shake briskly till they are done and begin to brown; dish your steak and lay the onions thickly on top; cover and let it stand five or six minutes, that the onions may impart their flavor to the meat. In helping your guests, inquire if they will take onions with the slices of steak put on their plates.

Roast Beef.

Wash the joint and wipe dry; then place it on a pan, with the fat and skin side up; put in a hot oven, and when the heat has started enough of the oil of the fat to baste with, open the oven, and drawing the pan toward you, take up a spoonful of grease and pour over the meat for a few times, closing the door immediately. This should be repeated four or five times during the process of roasting. When nearly done, sprinkle with salt and baste. Have ready a warm platter, and when the meat is dished, drain off the grease, carefully keeping back the rich, brown juice which has exuded from the meat.

This remaining gravy leave in the pan, placing it on the stove and adding about a gill of water; let it come to a boil, and then pour it over the meat. If a made gravy is preferred, more water should be added and a little flour. Salt hardens and toughens meat; therefore, in beef and mutton it should not be put on till it is cooked. It is also necessary to have the oven hot in order that the heat may quickly sear the surface, which will prevent the juice from escaping. It is obvious, if water is put in the pan, this quick searing can not be effected; water can not be raised above a certain temperature (its boiling point), while fat is susceptible of a much greater degree of heat, and therefore, as a basting agent, is preferable. Beef roasted before a fire has a flavor inexpressibly finer than that done in an oven.—*Home Messenger Receipt Book.*

Beef Loaf.
Mrs. S. A. Northway.

One and one-half pounds of lean steak chopped fine, two eggs, two tablespoons of butter, one tablespoon of salt, one teaspoon of pepper, one small cup of rolled crackers; mix well, form in a loaf, put bits of butter on top and bake. A fine relish for lunch or tea.

Prepared Meat.
Mrs. B. F. Wade.

Three pounds of steak chopped fine, two slices of bread well buttered, one teaspoon of salt, one-half of pepper, one teaspoon of sage, two eggs; mix well; make in a roll, and bake; when cold, slice. Very nice for tea or lunch.

MEATS.

Beef Rechauffe.
Mrs. C. S. Simonds.

Chop cold steak or roast; add gravy if you have it, if not, butter; season with salt and pepper; put in a saucepan or basin on the stove with a little boiling water; thicken slightly. When thoroughly heated spread upon hot buttered toast, and serve for breakfast.

Sweet-Breads.
Mrs. C. S. Simonds.

When they come into your possession put them immediately into cold water, ice water if you have it; let them lie a few minutes; then put in boiling water; boil twenty minutes; put them again into very cold water; when perfectly cold, take out and cut into slices one-fourth of an inch thick; dip in beaten egg and bread-crumbs, and fry in butter.

Sweet-Breads Stewed.

Wash, remove all the bits of skin, soak in salt and water one hour, then parboil; when half cooked take from the fire, cut into small pieces, stew in a little water till tender, add a piece of butter, a teaspoonful of salt, a teasponful of flour, and boil at once. Serve on toast very hot. Another way is to prepare as above and serve with tomato sauce.

Rissoles, (or Meat Balls.)
Miss Ada Simonds.

Hash cold mutton, beef or chicken, add one well beaten egg and a few bread crumbs; stir in the meat gravy and make into little round cakes; fry in butter.

Meat Croquettes.

Use cold roast beef or steak: chop it fine; season with pepper and salt; add $\frac{1}{3}$ the quantity of bread-crumbs, and moisten with a little milk. Have your hands floured; rub the meat into balls, dip them into beaten egg, then into fine pulverized cracker, and fry in butter; garnish with parsley.

Pounded Beef.

Boil a stew of twelve pounds of meat until it falls readily from the bone; pick it to pieces; mash gristle and all very fine and pick out all the hard bits. Set the liquor away till cool, then take off all the fat; return it to the stove and boil down to a pint and a half. While hot return the meat to it; add pepper and salt and any spice you choose. Let it boil a few times, stirring all the while.

Put into a mould or deep dish to cool. Use cold and cut in thin slices for tea or warm it for breakfast.

Beef Heart.

Wash carefully and stuff nicely, with dressing as for turkey; roast it about 1½ hours and serve with the gravy, which should be thickened with some of the dressing. It is very nice hashed.

Beef Liver.

Slice the liver and pour boiling water over it; wipe dry and cut it into very small pieces. Fry slices of fat salt pork until brown; take out the pork and fry the liver in the fat; cook thoroughly. When done pour a little water over the liver and thicken with a little flour and water, mixed smooth. Salt to taste.

To Boil a Tongue.

Soak it all night before using, and be careful to wash out the salt, which is put into various crevices to preserve it. Boil it in plenty of water from two and a half to three hours. Remove the skin before sending it to the table, and garnish with parsley.

Deviled Beef.

Take slices of cold roast beef, lay them on hot coals and broil; season with pepper and salt and serve while hot, with a small lump of butter on each piece.

Dried Beef in Cream.

Shave your beef very fine; pour over it boiling water; let it stand for a few minutes; pour this off and put on good rich cream; let it come to a boil. If you have not cream, use milk and butter and thicken with flour. Season with pepper and serve on toast or not, as you like.

Frizzled Beef.

Shave dried beef very fine and put in a hot frying-pan with a little butter; shake and stir until heated through. Season with pepper and serve in this way, or beat an egg light and stir in just before serving.

Scrambled Eggs with Beef.

Dried beef chipped very fine. Have some butter in the pan and when hot put in the beef; heat for a few minutes, stirring to prevent burning; break some eggs into a bowl, season, stir into the beef and cook a few minutes.

Minced Beef.
Mrs. N. E. French.

3½ lbs. raw beef chopped fine. 3 eggs. 6 soda crackers rolled. ⅔ cup sweet milk, salt and pepper. Make in a loaf and bake 1½ hours.

Meat Pie with Potato Crust. Very nice.
Mrs. B. W. Baldwin.

Remnants of all kinds of cold meat may be used for this. Remove all gristle and chop fine, season with salt and plenty of pepper. Put a layer of this in a buttered pudding dish, spread over it some catsup or prepared mustard if you like, then a layer of mashed cold potato, stick bits of butter all over this, a layer of meat again—and so on until ready for the crust. Make a crust,—allowing for 3 cups mashed potatoes—¾ cup sweet milk, 1 well beaten egg, a pinch of salt. Mix well, spread on top of meat, stick bits of butter all over it. Bake to a delicate brown ½ or three quarters of an hour.

Meat Pie.
Mrs. B. F. Wade.

Tak roast beef or steak, cut fine and lay with pepper, salt in bottom of dish, (an onion if one likes,) over this pour a cup of tomatoes and a little more pepper; over the top spread a thick layer of mashed potatoes. Bake in slow oven.

Meat or Chicken Dumplings.
Mrs. G. C. Lewis, Mt. Vernon.

1 pint of flour with 1½ teaspoon baking powder stirred through. One egg and one cup of sweet milk. Make all into a batter and drop by the spoonful into the kettle with the meat or chicken, and boil not more than twenty minutes. After the meat and dumplings are removed, thicken the gravy.

Roast Lamb.

Choose a hind quarter of lamb, stuff it with fine bread crumbs, pepper, salt, butter, and a little sage. Sew the flap firmly to keep in place, rub the outside with salt, pepper, butter, a little of the stuffing, and roast two hours. Eat with mint sauce.

Breaded Lamb Chops.

Grate plenty of stale bread, season with salt and pepper, have ready some well-beaten egg, have a spider with hot lard ready, take the chops one by one, dip into the egg, then into the bread crumbs; repeat it, as it will be found an improvement; then lay separately into the boiling lard, fry brown, and then turn. To be eaten with currant jelly or grape catsup.

Cutlets a la Duchesse.

Cut the neck of lamb (about two pounds) into cutlets, trim them and scrape the top of the bone clean, fry in butter and set away to cool. Put a piece of butter into a stew-pan with three mushrooms and a sprig of parsley, chop fine; stir over the fire until very hot, then pour over a cupful of white sauce—the yolks of three of four eggs well beaten. Stir constantly until as thick as cream, but do not let it boil. Dip each cutlet into it, covering thickly with the sauce, again set away to cool. Then egg and bread-crumb them. Fry lightly.

To Fry Lamb Steaks.

Dip each piece into well-beaten egg, cover with bread crumbs or corn meal, and fry in butter or new lard. Mashed potatoes and boiled rice are a necessary accompaniment. It is very nice to thicken the gravy with flour and butter, adding a little lemon juice, and pour it hot upon the steaks, and place the rice in spoonfuls around the dish to garnish it.

Spiced Lamb (Cold).

Boil a leg of lamb, adding to the water a handful of cloves and two or three sticks of cinnamon broken up. Boil four hours.

Stewed Lamb Chops.

Cut a loin of mutton into chops, cover with water and stew them until tender, keeping well covered except skimming. When done season with salt and pepper, and thicken the gravy with a little flour, stirred until smooth, with a piece of butter the size of a walnut. Have pieces of bread previously toasted, and pour the stew over them.

Mutton Chops.

Trim neatly, season, and dip each chop into a beaten egg, and then in cracker-crumbs; put into the oven in a dripping-pan with two spoonfuls of butter and a little water; baste frequently and bake until well browned.

Irish Stew.

Take mutton chops, cover well with water, and let them come to a boil; pour this off and add more water; then a lump of butter the size of an egg, two tablespoonfuls of flour, one teacupful of milk, season, potatoes, and two small onions. Boil until the potatoes are done.

Ragout.

Take pieces of mutton veal, beef, or rabbit, cut into any size or shape desired; heat a tablespoonful of drippings or lard in a saucepan, and when hot, fry the meat until almost done. Take out the meat and add a teaspoonful of flour, brown it, add a little lukewarm water, mix it well and then add a quart of boiling water; season with salt and cayenne pepper, add the meat, three or four onions, and six or seven potatoes, partially boiled before being put into the ragout; cover closely and stew until the vegetables are done. Take out the meat and vegetables and skim off all the fat from the gravy, season more if necessary and pour over the ragout and serve.

Spiced Veal.
Mrs. B. W. Baldwin.

Chop three pounds of veal steak and one thick slice of fat salt pork as fine as sausage meat; add three Boston crackers, rolled fine, three well beaten eggs, one-half teacupful of tomato catsup, one and one-half teaspoonfuls of fine salt, one teaspoonful of pepper, and one grated lemon. Mould into the form of a loaf of bread in small dripping-pan; cover with one rolled cracker, and baste often with a teacupful of hot water and two tablespoonfuls of melted butter (this makes it moist); bake three hours; make the day before using; slice very thin and garnish with slices of lemon and bits of parsley.

Potted Veal.
Mrs. B. W. Baldwin.

Mix well together three pounds of raw veal well chopped, eight tablespoonfuls of rolled crackers, three tablespoonfuls of cream or milk, one tablespoonful of pepper, one tablespoonful of salt, one grated nutmeg, and two eggs; fill a bread-pan, butter the top, sprinkle with more cracker, and bake three hours.

Veal Cutlets.
Mrs. B. W. Baldwin.

Trim off all fat, flatten with hammer, dip in beaten egg, then in Indian meal; have the butter hot, but not scorched, salt while frying. Fry until well done, adding butter to prevent burning.

Veal Cutlets.
Mrs. E. C. Wade.

Cut veal steak into pieces convenient for handling; dip in beaten egg, then in flour, and fry in butter; cook slowly, as veal needs to be cooked through; when done, remove from the spider, and make a gravy in the same with milk.

Veal Scallop.

Chop some cold roast or stewed veal very fine; put a layer on the bottom of a pudding-dish well buttered; season with pepper and salt. Next have a layer of fine-powdered crackers; wet with a little milk or some of the gravy from the meat. Proceed until the dish is full. Spread over all a thick layer of cracker-crumbs, seasoned with salt, and wet into a paste with milk and two beaten eggs. Stick bits of butter all over it, cover closely, and bake half an hour; then remove the cover and bake long enough to brown nicely. Do not get it too dry.

Croquette.

Take cold veal, chicken, or sweet-breads, a little of each, or separately; cut very fine a little fat and lean of ham, half the quantity of the whole of bread-crumbs, two eggs, butter the size of an egg, pepper, salt, and a little mustard. Knead like sausage meat, adding a little cream; form in any shape, dip in egg, and then roll in cracker-crumbs; fry in lard until a light brown. Dry them in the oven. Celery or mushrooms are an improvement.

Beef Omelet or Veal Loaf.
Mrs. W. H. Ruggles.

One pound of chopped steak, two eggs, piece of butter size of a hickory nut, one-half cup of rolled crackers, pepper, salt and sage; mix thoroughly and make into a roll; steam one-half hour and bake one-half hour.

Minced Veal.
Mrs. E. F. Abell.

To three pounds of veal chopped fine, add six grated crackers, one egg, a piece of butter the size of an egg, seasoned with nutmeg or sweet thyme, as you prefer; pepper and salt; make it into a loaf, place it in a pan lined with pork, lay over the top thin slices of pork, put a little water in the pan, and bake two hours.

Veal Pie.

Line a deep tin pan with a good crust; parboil the meat, and put it in, season high; nearly fill the pan with water in which the meat was parboiled. Sprinkle flour over, add a piece of butter, and cover with a tolerably thick crust. Chicken, clam or oyster may be made in the same manner. Oysters must not be cooked before putting into the pie.

MEATS.

To mix Sausage.
Mrs. Wm. Gibson.

3 pounds of salt to the 100 weight. ½ pound pepper. ½ pound sage. 2 ounces ginger.

Sausage.
Mrs. B. F. Wade.

36 lbs of meat, 48 teaspoonfuls of sage, 24 of pepper, 24 of salt.

To Season Sausages.
Mrs. Thomas Fricker.

To 10 lbs. meat add 1 heaping tablespoon pepper, 2 of salt and 3 of sage, and mix thoroughly.

Sausage.
Mrs. N. E. French.

1 heaping teaspoon salt, ½ spoon pepper, ½ spoon sage, ½ spoon summer savory, to 1 pound meat.

Bologna Sausage (cooked).

Two pounds lean beef; two pounds lean veal; two pounds lean pork; two pounds salt pork—not smoked; one pound beef suet; ten teaspoonfuls powdered mace; four pounds marjoram, parsley, savory and thyme—mixed; two teaspoonfuls cayenne pepper, and the same of black; one grated nutmeg; one teaspoonful cloves; one minced onion; salt to taste. Chop or grind the meat and suet; season, and stuff into beef-skins; tie these up; prick each in several places to allow the escape of the steam; put into hot—not boiling water, and heat gradually to the boiling point. Cook slowly for one hour; take out the skins and lay them to dry in the sun, upon clean, sweet straw or hay. Rub the outside of the skins with oil or melted butter, and hang in a cool, dry cellar. If you mean to keep it more than a week, rub pepper or pounded ginger upon the outside. You can wash it off before sending to the table. This is eaten without further cooking. Cut in round slices and lay sliced lemon around the edge of the dish, as many like to squeeze a few drops upon the sausage before eating.

Scrapple.

Take hogs heads, or any part will do, have the meat half fat and half lean, boil it until very tender, then chop very fine, put back in same water, add salt, pepper and summer savory to suit taste, boil altogether and thicken with corn meal, when cool cut in slices and fry as mush in butter.

Ham Toast.
Mrs. E. C. Wade.

Take pieces of cooked ham chopped fine; to each tablespoonful add yolk of 1 egg, and 1 tablespoonful sweet cream; salt and pepper; heat this mixture and spread on hot buttered toast; Serve quickly. Boiled tongue is equally good prepared in this way.

Ham Toast.
Mrs. S. A. Northway.

Mince cold ham finely, to 1 pint of mince put 2 tablespoons of cream or fresh rich milk; boil this 5 minutes, prepare well buttered slices of toast: and spread the mince on them, strew over this well grated bread crumbs, a little parsley, and some small pieces of butter. Brown in a quick oven and serve hot.

Baked Ham.

A ham of 16 pounds to be boiled three hours, then skin and rub in half a pound of brown sugar, cover with breadcrumbs and bake two hours.

Pork Steaks, Broiled.

Trim, season and roll them in melted butter and breadcrumbs; broil them over a moderate fire until thoroughly done. Make a sauce of five tablespoonfuls of vinegar and half a teacupful of stock; let it boil, and thicken with a little flour. Strain, and then add pepper and some pickles chopped fine.

To Fry Apples and Pork Chops.

Season the chops with salt and pepper and a little powdered sage and sweet marjoram; dip them into beaten egg and then into beaten bread-crumbs. Fry about twenty minutes, or until they are done. Put them on a hot dish; pour off part of the gravy into another pan, to make a gravy to serve with them, if you choose. Then fry apples which you have sliced about two-thirds of an inch thick, cutting them around the apple so that the core is in the center of each piece. When they are browned on one side and partly cooked, turn them carefully with a pancake turner, and let them finish cooking; dish around the chops or on a separate dish.

Spare Ribs Broiled.

Crack the bones and broil over a clear fire, taking care that the fire is not hot enough to scorch them.

Mint Sauce.

Wash the mint very clean; pick the leaves from the stalk, and chop them fine; pour onto them vinegar enough to moisten the mint well; add fine sugar to sweeten.

Celery Sauce.

Pick and wash two heads of celery; cut them into pieces one inch long, and stew them in a pint of water with one teaspoonful of salt, until the celery is tender. Rub a large spoonful of butter and a spoonful of flour well together; stir this into a pint of cream; put in the celery, and let it boil up once. Serve hot with boiled poultry.

Tomato Sauce.

Stew one-half dozen tomatoes with a little chopped parsley; salt and pepper to taste; strain, and when it commences to boil add a spoonful of flour, stirred smooth with a tablespoonful of butter. When it boils take up.

Tomato Sauce.

Stew one can of tomatoes, one small onion, for twenty minutes, and then strain through a sieve. Put an ounce and a half of butter into a saucepan, and when it boils, dredge in an ounce and a half of flour. When thoroughly cooked, pour in the tomatoes.

Tomato Sauce.

One can of tomatoes boiled down and strained; rub together one heaping teaspoonful of flour, one tablespoonful of butter, and a little salt, with a very little cayenne pepper, and stir into the tomatoes; then let all come to a boil.

Cranberry Sauce.

One quart of cranberries, one quart of water, and one pound of white sugar; make a sirup of the water and sugar. After washing the berries clean, and picking out all poor ones, drop them into the boiling sirup, let them cook from fifteen to twenty minutes. They are very nice strained.

Egg Sauce.

Three ounces of butter, beaten with one ounce of flour; stir into it one pint of boiling water; salt and pepper. Cook fifteen minutes; pour into sauce-boat, having hard-boiled eggs, sliced or chopped, in it.

Oyster Sauce.

One pint of oysters boiled three or four minutes in their own liquor. Stir in two tablespoonfuls of butter rolled in a spoonful of flour, the juice of half a lemon with pepper and salt to taste. Heat a teacupful of milk, pour into the oysters and turn at once into the sauce-boat.

SALADS.

Chicken Salad.
Mrs. E. H. Way.

Take two chickens, boil until tender; when cold, skin them, picking the meat from the bones, and chop fine; use about one-third more celery than chicken.

For the Dressing.

Three eggs and one-half cup of butter; rub well together, add black and cayenne pepper and mustard; pour on this mixture one pint of vinegar; let it boil and cool before putting on the chicken and celery. Boil six eggs hard, chop the whites, rub the yolks to a cream, put them in the dressing before pouring over the chicken.

Chicken Salad.
Mrs. B. W. Baldwin.

All the meat of a tender chicken, two-thirds of its weight of celery. For dressing, yolks of two raw and two hard boiled eggs, one large tablespoonful of dry mustard, stirring in one direction; add a little sweet oil until one-third of a bottle is added; juice of one lemon, then more oil, in all two-thirds of a bottle, a little vinegar, a teaspoonful or more of salt; make very slowly, and stir a long time; will be very white and nice, very nice for salad of any kind.

Chicken Salad.
Mrs. J. A. Howells.

Boil until very tender three chickens and one pound of veal; chop all together until fine; make a dressing of the yolks of four eggs boiled twenty minutes; rub smooth; add three teaspoonfuls of English mustard, two teaspoonfuls of salt, three tablespoonfuls of salad oil, one tablespoonful of white sugar, two-thirds of a pint of strong vinegar; chop fine and add three-fourths the bulk of celery.

In making chicken salad one-third veal boiled and chopped with the chicken, can be used with good effect. When celery cannot be got, crisp cabbage or lettuce, seasoned with celery seed pounded, or celery vinegar can be substituted.

Salmon Salad.

For a pound can of California salmon, garnished with lettuce, make a dressing of one small teacup of vinegar, butter half the size of an egg, one teaspoon of Colman's mustard, one-half teaspoonful of cayenne pepper, one-half teaspoonful of salt, one teaspoonful of sugar, two eggs; when cold, add one-half teacup of cream and pour over the salmon.

Sydney Smith's Receipt for Salad Dressing.

Two boiled potatoes, strained through a kitchen sieve,
Softness and smoothness to the salad give;
Of mordant mustard take a single spoon—
Distrust the condiment that bites too soon;
Yet deem it not, though man of taste, a fault,
To add a double quantity of salt.
Four times the spoon, with oil of Lucca crown,
And twice with vinegar procured from town;
True taste requires it, and your poet begs
The pounded yellow of two well-boiled eggs.
Let onion atoms lurk within the bowl,
And, scarce suspected, animate the whole;
And lastly, in the flavored compound toss
A magic teaspoonful of anchovy sauce.
Oh, great and glorious! oh, herbaceous meat!
'T would tempt the dying anchorite to eat;
Back to the world he'd turn his weary soul,
And plunge his fingers in the salad bowl.

Cabbage Salad.
Mrs. N. E. French.

Cut the cabbage fine, and salt to your taste, put sufficient vinegar on to moisten it, beat the yolks of 2 eggs, and ½ pint of milk, one teaspoonful of mustard, one of sugar, pepper to suit taste. Set it on the stove and stir until it thickens, when cold pour it on the cabbage.

Egg Salad.
Mrs. H. L. Hervey.

When cold cut twelve hard-boiled eggs in halves, remove the yolks, keeping the whites unbroken, rub the yolks fine and smooth as possible, work in a tablespoon of butter, season to taste, add a little celery or lettuce cut very fine, and two small teaspoons of mustard wet with vinegar, mix all together into a smooth paste, if not moist enough add more vinegar, fill the whites, garnish with celery or parsley tops, and it makes a nice dish for tea.

GAME.

Broiled Venison Steak.

Broil quickly over a clear fire, and when sufficiently done pour over two tablespoonfuls of currant jelly, melted with a piece of butter. Pepper and salt to season. Eat while hot, on hot plates.

To Cook Venison.

Broil as you would a beefsteak, rare. Have ready a gravy of butter, pepper and salt, and a very little water. Heat the gravy without boiling it. Score the steak all over, put it in the gravy and cover tight; keep hot enough to steam the meat, and send in a covered dish to table.

Pigeon Compote.

Truss six pigeons as for boiling. Grate the crumbs of a small loaf of bread, scrape one pound of fat bacon, chop thyme, parsley, and onion and lemon — peel fine — and season with salt and pepper; mix it up with two eggs; put this force-meat into the craws of the pigeons, lard the breasts and fry brown; place them in a stewpan with some beef stock and stew them three-quarters of an hour, thicken with a piece of butter rolled in flour. Serve with forcemeat balls around the dish and strain the gravy on to the pigeons.

To Roast Wild Fowl.

The flavor is best preserved without stuffing. Put pepper, salt and a piece of butter into each. Wild fowl require much less dressing than tame. They should be served of a fine color with a rich brown gravy. To take o the fishy taste, which wild fowl sometimes have, put an onion, salt and hot water into the dripping pan, and baste them for the first ten minutes with this, then take away the pan and baste constantly with butter.

To Roast Partridges, Pheasants or Quails.

Pluck, singe, draw and truss them, season with salt and pepper, roast for about half an hour in a brisk oven, basting often with butter. When done place on a dish together with breadcrumbs fried brown and arranged in small heaps. Gravy should be served in a tureen apart.

To Broil Quail or Woodcock.

After dressing, split down the back, sprinkle with salt

and pepper, and lay them on a gridiron, the inside down. Broil slowly at first. Serve with cream gravy.

To Roast Wild Duck or Teal.

After dressing, soak them over night in salt and water, to draw out the fishy taste. Then in the morning put them into fresh water, changing several times before roasting. Stuff or not, as desired. Serve with currant jelly.

Pigeon Pie.

Dress and wash clean, split down the back, and then proceed as for chicken pie.

Roast Pigeons.

When cleaned and ready for roasting, fill the bird with a stuffing of bread crumbs, a spoonful of butter, a little salt and nutmeg, and three oysters to each bird (some prefer chopped apple). They must be well basted with melted butter, and require thirty minutes' careful cooking. In the autumn they are best, and should be full grown.

To Roast Pigeons.

They should be dressed while fresh. If young, they will be ready for roasting in twelve hours. Dress carefully, and after making clean, wipe dry and put into each bird a small piece of butter dipped in cayenne. Truss the wings over the back and roast in a quick oven, keeping them constantly basted with butter. Serve with brown gravy. Dish them with young water-cresses.

Fried Rabbit.

After the rabbit has been thoroughly cleaned and washed, put it into boiling water and let boil for about ten minutes; drain, and when cold, cut it into joints, dip into beaten egg, and then into fine bread-crumbs, seasoned with salt and pepper. When all are ready fry them in butter over a moderate fire fifteen minutes, thicken the gravy with an ounce of butter and a small teaspoonful of flour, give it a minute's boil, stir in two tablespoonfuls of cream, dish the rabbit, pour the sauce under it, and serve quickly.

Stewed Rabbit.

Skin and clean the rabbit, cut into pieces, put one-fourth of a pound of butter into a stewpan and turn the pieces of rabbit about in it until nicely browned; take out the meat, add one pint of boiling water to the butter, one tablespoonful of flour stirred to a paste in cold water, one tablespoonful of salt, and a little grated onion if liked; let this boil up, add the meat, stew slowly till the rabbit is tender. Serve hot.

VEGETABLES.

Have your vegetables fresh as possible. Wash them thoroughly. Lay them in cold water until ready to use them.

Vegetables should be put to cook in boiling water and salt. Never let them stand after coming off the fire; put them instantly into a colander over a pot of boiling water, if you have to keep them back from dinner.

Peas, beans and asparagus, if young, will cook in twenty-five or thirty minutes. They should be boiled in a good deal of salt water.

Cauliflower should be wrapped in a cloth when boiled, and served with drawn butter. Potato water is thought to be unhealthy; therefore do not boil potatoes in soup, but in another vessel, and add them to it when cooked.

A lump of bread about the size of a billiard ball, tied up in a linen bag and placed in the pot in which greens are boiling, will absorb the gasses which often times send such an unpleasant odor to the regions above.

Lima Beans.

Shell, wash, and put into boiling water with a little salt; when boiled tender, drain and season them, and either dress with cream, or large lump of butter, and let simmer for a few moments.

Stewed Potatoes.

Slice cold boiled potatoes quite thin, place in a shallow pan, cover with milk, stir them so they will not burn, keep them covered closely; for potatoes enough for 6 persons, mix 1 teaspoon of flour with a little cold milk to a smooth paste, add this and let them cook thoroughly for 5 minutes, then add salt and butter, do not let them stand over the fire long after the salt is added as the milk will curdle.

Lyonnaise Potatoes.

Put a pint of milk in a frying-pan; add a piece of butter the size of a butter-nut, some salt and pepper; let it boil; take a heaping teaspoonful of corn-starch, mix with a little cold milk, add, stirring till it thickens; have six or seven good-sized peeled potatoes, (boiled or baked the day before,) cut them in small pieces, put all together; let cook fifteen minutes, stirring to prevent burning.

Potato Puff.

2 large cups of cold mashed potato, 2 tablespoons melted butter beaten to a white cream, then add 2 well-beaten eggs, 1 teacup of cream or milk and little salt. Beat well, pour into deep dish, and bake in quick oven a nice brown.

Saratoga Chips.

Pare and slice on a slaw cutter raw potatoes into cold water, then spread them between folds of cloth until dry, and fry a few at a time in boiling lard, salt as they are taken out. Very crisp and nice.

Boiled Potatoes.

Potatoes in the spring begin to shrivel and should be soaked in cold water several hours before cooking. Put them over the fire in cold water (without salt), and, when done, drain off the water, returning them to the fire for a minute or two, but not long enough to endanger burning; then throw in a little salt; take hold of the handle and toss the kettle in such a way that the potatoes will be thrown up and down. When they look white and floury they are ready to dish for the table. New potatoes should always be put into BOILING water, and it is better to prepare them only just in time for cooking.—*Home Messenger Receipt Book.*

Fried Corn.
Mrs. J. A. Howells.

For a family of five, take one dozen plump ears of sweet corn, with a thin sharp knife cut off the top of the kernels, then scrape all the pulp and juice from the cob. Take a thin small slice of salt pork, cut into small bits and fry to a crisp, put the corn into this, season with pepper and salt, and fry twenty minutes.

Corn Oysters.
Mrs. E. C. Wade.

2 dozen ears of corn; 1 tablespoon butter; 1 egg, pepper and salt; ½ teacup sweet milk.

Use only the pulp of the corn, pressing it out from the skin with a fork. Beat the egg, mix and bake.

Corn Oyster Cakes.
Miss Ada Simonds.

Take 4 or 5 ears soft sweet corn; run a knife through each row of kernels and press out the contents; add two beaten eggs, a little salt and enough flour to make the batter thick; then fry as other pancakes.

Baked Beans.
Mrs. Jas. Whitmore.

Look over at night 1 quart of beans, cover them with plenty of water, and let them stand until morning. Then take them from the water, and put into a gallon crock. Lay on top a piece of fat salt pork 3 inches square, gash the rind, add one teaspoonful molasses, ¼ teaspoonful soda, and water enough to cover. Bake slowly five hours, occasionally adding a little water.

Baked Pork and Beans.
Mrs. E. A. Sheldon.

Soak beans over night, place in iron kettle with piece of pork in center, cover with water and a snug lid; cook 5 hours in a moderate oven, as the water boils off fill up, till an hour before using, then remove the lid and brown them.

Baked Cabbage.

Cook as for boiled cabbage, drain and let get cold, chop fine, add two beaten eggs, tablespoon butter, pepper, salt, three tablespoons cream, stir well and bake in buttered dish till brown. Serve hot.

Cheese Straws.
Mrs. Bostwick.

¼ pound of grated cheese, ¼ pound flour, 2 oz. butter, a little salt, a pinch of black pepper; moisten with water suflicient to roll very thin, cut like straws, bake slow, they can be twisted three together if preferred.

Salsify.

Wash and scrape the roots, and unless they are to be cooked immediately, keep them covered with water, as they blacken very soon. Slice and boil, letting the water boil out when they are tender. Make a gravy over them with milk, or better still, cream, season with butter, salt and pepper, thicken to the consistency of cream, and dish in saucers. Or you may serve on toast if preferred. Some slices of dried beef added will give a richer flavor.

How to Cook "String Beans."

"German wax" are the best, as they need no stringing—simply removing each end and cutting into short pieces and boil for two or more hours, as long cooking improves their flavor. After boiling a few minutes add a teaspoon or more of soda, and when the beans are tender, pour off that water, and for the remainder of the cooking use as little water as possible, salting a little while before the cream, or milk and butter is added, and serve soon as that is *hot*—never allowing the milk to boil.

Baked Egg Plant.

Cut in halves a nice smooth egg plant; scoop out the center, leaving with the skin about one-third of an inch; chop the inside of the egg plant very fine, two ripe tomatoes, one onion, some bread-crumbs, a little parsley, and green pepper—onion and pepper to be chopped separately very fine—salt, butter, and very little pepper; mix very smooth, put in the shell, butter on top, and bake about one-half hour.

Asparagus.

Cut up the stalks in half inch lengths discarding the tough ends; cover with boiling and cook twenty-five minutes: do not pour away the water unless you have too much; season highly with butter salt and pepper. Spread upon hot buttered toast and serve immediately.

Another way to prepare the same vegetable:—When boiled soft, pour off the water and add one or more teacupfuls of milk, according to the quantity; let it come again to the boiling point; season with salt, pepper and butter, and serve in sauce plates.

Fried Egg Plant.

Pare and slice them, then sprinkle each slice with salt and let them stand for about one hour with a weight on them, then dip into egg well beaten, then flour and fry light brown in lard and butter.

Turnips.

Pare and cut into pieces; put them into boiling water well salted, and boil until tender; drain thoroughly and then mash and add a piece of butter, pepper, and salt to taste, and a small teaspoonful of sugar. Stir until they are thoroughly mixed, and serve.

Escalloped Onions.

Boil till tender 6 large onions, separate them with a spoon, then place in a pudding dish a layer of onions, then layer of bread-crumbs seasoned with pepper, salt, butter, and moistened with milk. Set in the oven and brown.

Macaroni with Cheese.

Boil macaroni in water with a little salt $\frac{1}{4}$ of an hour, then drain off water and add milk, and boil till done. Cover pudding dish with layer of macaroni with butter, then grated cheese, bread-crumbs, pepper, butter, and thus alternately until full. Bake 15 minutes in quick oven and serve hot.

Cauliflower.

Trim off outside leaves, and put into boiling water well salted, first placing in cloth bag, boil till tender, and serve with cream or milk, and butter.

Parsnip Fritters.
Mrs. B. F. Bowman, Jr.

Pare and scrape, cut in slices, boil, mash and season, same as mashed potatoes. Instead of putting in milk put in a well-beaten egg, make into small cakes, and fry in half lard and butter a light brown.

Fried Parsnips.

Scrape, cut into strips, and boil until tender in salted water; drain and dip into batter, made with one egg beaten light, one-half cup milk, and flour enough to make a batter, and fry in hot butter or lard.

Spinach.

Spinach requires good washing and close picking. Boil twenty minutes in boiling water, drain, season with butter, pepper, and salt; garnish the dish with slices of hard-boiled eggs.

To Cook Mushrooms.
Mrs. J. A. Howells.

Have nothing to do with them until you can judge between true and false. The TRUE are most plenty in August or September. The top is a dirty white, the underside pink or salmon, changing to a russet or brown soon after gathered. Those white above and below are poisonous, and the latter sport all colors. To boil mushrooms, peel and boil 10 or 16 minutes in little water, and season with butter, pepper and salt.

French Mushrooms Canned.

Pour off the liquid, pour over them a little cream, season, and let them simmer for a short time. To be served on broiled beefsteak.

Mushrooms Broiled.

Gather them fresh, pare, and cut off the stems, dip them in melted butter, season with salt and pepper, broil them on both sides over a clear fire; serve on toast.

Macaroni with Oysters.

Boil macaroni in salt water, after which draw through a colander; take a deep earthen dish or tin, put in alternate layers of macaroni and oysters, sprinkle the layers of macaroni with grated cheese; bake until brown.

Stewed Macaroni.

Boil two ounces of macaroni in water, drain well, put into a sauce-pan one ounce of butter, mix with one tablespoonful of flour, moisten with four tablespoonfuls of veal or beef stock, one gill of cream; salt and white pepper to taste; put in the macaroni, let it boil up, and serve while hot.

Macaroni as a Vegetable.

Simmer one-half pound of macaroni in plenty of water till tender, but not broken; strain off the water. Take the yolks of five and the whites of two eggs, one-half pint of cream; white meat and ham chopped very fine, three spoonfuls of grated cheese. Season with salt and pepper; heat all together, stirring constantly. Mix with the macaroni, put into a buttered mold and steam one hour.

Scalloped Tomatoes.

Butter an earthen dish, then put in a layer of fresh tomatoes, sliced and peeled, and a few rinds of onion (one large onion for the whole dish), then cover with a layer of bread-crumbs, with a little butter, salt and pepper. Repeat this process until the dish is full. Bake for an hour in a pretty hot oven.

Browned Tomatoes.

Take large round tomatoes and halve them, place them the skin side down in a frying-pan in which a very small quantity of butter and lard has been previously melted, sprinkle them with salt and pepper, and dredge well with flour. Place the pan on a hot part of the fire, and let them brown thoroughly; then stir, and let them brown again, and so on until they are quite done. They lose their acidity, and their flavor is superior to stewed tomatoes.

To Broil Tomatoes.

Take large round tomatoes, wash and wipe, and put them in a gridiron over lively coals, the stem side down. When brown, turn them and let them cook till quite hot through. Place them on a hot dish, and send quickly to the table, when each one may season for himself with pepper, salt and butter.

Baked Tomatoes.

Fill a deep pan (as many as will cover the bottom) with ripe tomatoes; round out a hole in the center of each; fill up with bread-crumbs, butter, pepper and salt; put a teacup of water in the pan. Bake till brown; send to the table hot.

EGGS.

Fried Eggs.

Put a very little butter in each cup of a gem pan, which should be hot enough to hiss; break an egg in each cup, and fry till the eggs are hard as desired.

This is a quick and easy way of frying eggs, as they preserve the shape of the cup. It makes a very pretty dish.

Boiled Eggs.

The most delicate way of preparing is by pouring over them boiling water, and let them stand fifteen minutes, closely covered. If kept hot without boiling, the white becomes very white and delicate. An egg cooked the day it is laid requires a longer time to cook than one that is a day or two old.

Scrambled Eggs.

Have a spider hot and buttered; break the eggs into a dish, being careful not to break the yolks; slip them into the spider, add a very little salt, with butter the size of a nutmeg for a half dozen eggs, or three tablespoonfuls of rich cream. When the eggs begin to whiten, stir carefully from the bottom, until cooked to suit. The yolks and whites should be separated, though stirred together.

Baked Eggs.

Break as many eggs as needed in a buttered sauce-pan, with a small piece of butter on each, with pepper and salt, and bake till the whites are set. Are far more delicate than fried eggs.

Egg Baskets.

Boil as many eggs as needed quite hard; put into cold water, then cut into halves; remove the yolks and rub to a paste with melted butter; pepper and salt, then take cold roast chicken or turkey, which may be on hand, chop fine and mix well with the yolk paste, moistening it with melted butter and gravy, and heat it well over hot water. Cut off a small slice from the end of the empty halves so they will stand firmly, and fill them with the paste. Place close together on a dish or platter, and pour over them the rest of the gravy. A few spoons of cream or milk is an improvement.

Stuffed Eggs.

Boil the eggs hard, remove shells and cut in two either way, as preferred; mix with the removed yolks, pepper, salt, and a little mustard, if liked, cold chicken, ham or tongue chopped fine, and a little butter; stuff the cavities, smooth them and put halves together again. For picnics, wrap them in tissue paper to keep together.

To Poach Eggs.

Lay small muffin-rings in the water and drop an egg in each ring, and the egg will be smooth and the shape of the ring.

Omelet.
Mrs. B. W. Baldwin.

Beat six eggs very light, the whites to a stiff frost that will stand alone, the yolks to a smooth, thick batter; add to 'the yolks a small cupful of milk, pepper and salt to taste; lastly, stir in the whites lightly; have ready in a hot frying-pan a good lump of butter; when it hisses pour in the mixture and set over a clear fire. Do not stir it, but contrive, as the eggs set, to slip a broad-bladed knife under the omelet. When done, lay a hot plate, bottom upwards, on the pan, turn it over brown side up. Eat immediately. This is very fluffy and nice, but gentlemen usually prefer one a little more solid.

Omelet.
Mrs. B. W. Baldwin.

Allow one tablespoonful of cold water to each egg; break the eggs into a bowl, add salt, pepper and water; simply stir it two or three times, or enough to break the yolks; heat a good lump of butter in the frying-pan; when hot, carefully pour in the omelet. When it begins to set in the middle, fold together by a dexterous turn of the frying-pan. Cook to a delicate brown. The water will prevent its being leathery. Finely minced ham or oysters is a delicate addition to a plain omelet.

Egg Sandwiches.

Butter the bread and line the sandwiches with slices of hard-boiled eggs, slightly salted and peppered. Throw the the eggs as soon as boiled into very cold water, and leave them to cool there. This will prevent the yolks from turning blue-black.

BREAD.

Selecting Flour.

First look to the color; if it is white, with a yellowish-colored tint, buy it; if it is white, with a bluish cast, or with white specks in it, refuse it. Second, examine its adhesiveness—wet and knead a little of it between your fingers—if it works soft and sticky, it is poor. Third, throw a little lump of dried flour against a smooth surface, if it falls like powder, it is bad. Fourth, squeeze some of the flour tightly in your hand, if it retains the shape given by the pressure, that, too, is a good sign. It is safe to buy flour that will stand all these tests.

Yeast.

Pare and grate one dozen small potatoes, add one teacupful of sugar, one-half teacupful of salt, one tablespoonful of ginger; pour on to this while stirring, one quart of boiling water; boil a small handful of hops, strain and add to the above; when cool, add a teacupful of yeast. Let this raise twenty-four hours. Bottle tight and set in a cool place.

Dry Hop Yeast.
Miss Fannie Dean.

Take two handfuls of fresh hops, put in a kettle and pour over them one quart of boiling water; boil about twenty minutes, stirring occasionally; then strain the liquid boiling hot into two cups of flour, and put it in. When cooled to about milk heat, add yeast sufficient to raise it, let stand till light, then mix it stiff with corn meal, and make into cakes; spread on a board in the shade to dry, turning over occasionally while drying. When thoroughly dried, tie up tight in a paper bag, and you will have yeast that will keep three or four months.

Hop Yeast.
Mrs. H. L. Hervey.

Two quarts of potatoes after they are pared; boil quick in plenty of water, mash very fine after they are done; take one-half pint of hops, pour over them three pints of water; let them boil about five minutes, then strain over the potatoes, and stir until the water and potatoes are well mixed, then add one-half teacupful of salt, one of sugar;

then set in a cool place until it is just warm, then stir in one teacupful of good yeast, and it will be ready for use as soon as light. In winter keep in a warm place until it rises, then close up tightly and keep cool. Do not use iron to cook the potatoes or hops in, as it makes the yeast dark.

Dry Hop Yeast.
Mrs. H. L. Hervey.

Make a sponge, same as for bread, of fresh hop yeast; as soon as light, stir in enough corn meal to thicken, so with a very little flour it can be kneaded into cakes one-half inch thick; spread on boards to dry; turn them twice a day. Do not put them in the sun or by the fire while drying, and keep covered with a thin cloth. When perfectly dry, tie up tightly in a paper bag, or put in glass fruit jars and keep in a cool, dry place.

Railroad Yeast for Salt Rising.
Mrs. B. W. Baldwin.

One teacup of middlings or Graham flour, one teaspoon of ginger, one-fourth teaspoon of salt, one-fourth of soda; make into batter with boiling water. Let it stand one day in a warm place; next morning put into rising made the usual way.

Salt Rising Bread.
Mrs. B. F. Bowman, Jr.

Put in a pint bowl one teaspoonful of salt, one-half teaspoonful of sugar, one-half teaspoonful of ginger, a piece of salaratus the size of a pea; turn on a teacupful of boiling water, cool it with milk lukewarm; stir in flour; make the batter a little thicker than you would for pancakes. Set the rising at night, and place on a heated soap stone. As soon as it is light in the morning, make your sponge, two-thirds of a quart of milk or water, or equal parts of each, and enough flour to make it stiff as you would for yeast bread; then put in your rising, and stir it briskly. Sprinkle one teacupful of flour over the top, cover with a newspaper or towel, then set it over a kettle half full of hot water (let the kettle remain on the stove); place two small sticks over the kettle, then put on your bread-pan. Be careful and do not let the water get so hot so that it will scald your sponge; it will stand considerable heat, but not enough to scald it. When it gets real light, mold into loaves, and let rise again; put in the warming closet until the loaves begin to crack across the top and look very light; then bake.

White Bread.
Mrs. C. S. Simonds.

To make 3 loaves of bread, pare and boil 6 or 8 small potatoes; mash free from lumps and pour on 1 quart boiling water; this amount should include the water in which the potatoes are boiled. Stir in while still at scalding heat 1 handful flour; if potatoes are not used 3 handfuls of flour should be scalded. When the sponge becomes lukewarm add flour enough to make a moderately thick batter, and $\frac{1}{3}$ of a teacupful of good yeast. If set in the evening the sponge should stand over night where it will not become chilled and should be mixed early in the morning. Add to it 1 tablespoonful softened butter, $\frac{1}{2}$ teaspoonful salt and if overlight a "pinch" of soda. Transfer the sponge from the dish in which it has stood over night to a large bowl containing about 3 quarts flour. Mix with the hands until the dough is thick enough to knead; it is desirable to have a little more flour in the bowl than you wish to work into the dough. Do not make the dough stiffer than is absolutely necessary for handling upon the moulding board upon which it should be kneaded with well floured hands until it is quite smooth and springs beneath the hands. Set in a warm place to rise; when light, mould down and knead. It may now be moulded into loaves, but will be improved by a third rising and kneading. When light enough for baking, gash the loaves slightly with a sharp knife to prevent binding of the crust. Bake $\frac{3}{4}$ of an hour in an oven which is hot when the loaves are put in; the fire should decrease when they begin browning.

French Rolls.
Mrs. U. Z. Canfield, Buffalo.

Take 1 pint of very light bread-dough, $\frac{1}{2}$ pint sweet milk, 1 tablespoonful of lard, soda the size of a pea; boil milk, lard and soda together, and pour over the dough; add two tablespoonfuls sugar, 1 teaspoonful of salt; mix thoroughly, then add flour to make a soft dough. Set in a warm place until very light, then roll about $\frac{1}{2}$ inch thick, spread a little lard over the top, and cut out with cake cutter; double nearly half over, put in pans, do not let them touch. Let them rise and bake 15 minutes.

Parker House Rolls.
Mrs. S. A. Northway.

2 quarts flour, 1 teaspoonful salt, 2 teaspoonfuls lard, 1 pint scalded milk, $\frac{1}{2}$ cup yeast, a scant $\frac{1}{2}$ teacupful of white

sugar. Mix well the flour, lard and salt; when the milk has cooled to lukewarm, then add the yeast and sugar, make a deep hole in the flour, pour in the mixture, just covering it lightly with flour; let it rise 7 or 8 hours, then mix as soft bread. Roll out, cut round and lop over, putting a lump of butter between, then let them rise in a pan, and bake.

Parker House Rolls.
Mrs. E. F. Abell.

2 quarts flour; 1 pint milk; ½ teacup yeast; ½ teacup lard; ¼ teacup sugar; 1 teaspoon salt. Boil the milk and let the lard melt in it; sift the flour into a deep dish and make a hole in the centre; put in the yeast, then sugar and salt, and add the milk after it has cooled. Let it stand without mixing all night; in the morning mix and mold. Put back in the dish and rise; after dinner mold again: roll half an inch thick, cut with round cutter, and fold together; let them rise until time to bake for supper. In summer if put to rise after breakfast they will be light enough to bake for tea. When nearly done brush the tops lightly with a cloth dipped in milk.

Raised Biscuit. Nice.
Mrs. N. E. French.

To 1 pint of potato sponge add in the morning a little pulverized sugar, 1 pint warm milk or water, a little flour; let stand until light, then add 1 cup butter, 1 egg or two; make soft and mould well. Will make 45 or 50 biscuit.

Sweet Rusk.

Make a sponge with 1 pint warm milk, 2 tablespoons yeast, and flour for a thin batter and let rise over night. In the morning add ½ cup butter, 2 eggs, 1 cup sugar, teaspoon salt well mixed together, and flour to make soft dough. Mould small size and let rise very light. After baking, wet the tops with molasses and water.

Rusk.
Mrs. S. A. Northway.

3 cups of milk, 1 cup of yeast, 1 cup sugar, and a little salt, make a batter as for bread, when light, add one cup more of sugar, 1 cup of lard and butter together, 2 eggs, leaving out the white of one, a little nutmeg; knead very soft, when light mould and put into tins like biscuit, when light again, beat the white of the egg, and with a piece of cloth wet them over just before placing them in the oven. Bake 20 minutes. This will make 30 rusks.

Brown Bread.
Mrs. M. E. Galpin.

1 cup molasses, 1 teaspoon soda, stir these into one quart milk, and thicken with equal parts corn meal and graham to the consistency of cake batter, ½ teaspoon salt. Boil in a mould 3 hours.

Brown Bread.
Jane Curtis.

1 pint of bread crumbs soaked, 1 cup of scalded meal, 1 cup of light bread sponge, ½ cup of molasses; mix these together, place in a pan of flour and work into a loaf. Let rise and bake ¾ of an hour.

Boston Brown Bread.
Mrs. H. L. Hervey.

1½ cups of flour, 1½ cups of meal, 1½ cups of rye or graham flour, 2½ cups of sour milk, 1 teaspoonful soda. Steam 2½ hours, then put in a moderately hot oven for 1½ hours, or until it is a light brown.

Boston Brown Bread.
Mrs. S. A. Northway.

3 cups sweet milk, 2 cups of sour milk, 4 cups of corn meal, 2 of flour, 1 of syrup, small tablespoonful of soda, the same of salt. Steam 2 hours and bake ½ hour.

Graham Bread.
Mrs. E. A. Sheldon.

1 quart of water, 1 tablespoonful of salt, ½ cup of sugar, 1 cup of yeast, enough graham flour to make a stiff batter; sponge at night and leave in a warm place to rise. In the morning turn into a pan without stirring it down. Let stand ½ hour, and bake 1 hour.

Graham Bread.
Mrs. E. L. Sampson.

From your bread sponge take 1½ pints, add 1 quart water, 1 cup sugar, a little salt, mix well together; add graham enough to make a batter as thick as you can stir with a spoon.

Graham Bread.
Miss Ada Simonds.

For 1 loaf scald 1 handful of white flour with 1 pint of boiling water. When cool add graham flour until as thick as white sponge and stir in 1 tablespoonful of yeast. When light add a generous pinch of salt, a piece of butter half the size of a hen's egg, and a tablespoonful of molasses. Then with one hand in the flour and the other in the sponge add flour until you can lift it readily from the pan; it does not require kneading and must not be made as stiff as white dough. If a larger loaf is desired a little milk may be added to the sponge in the final mixing. Transfer to the baking tin and set to rise. A loaf of this size will bake in half an hour in a moderately quick oven.

Corn Bread.
Mrs. A. M. Williams.

5 cups of meal, 3 of flour, 2 of sour milk, 4 of sweet milk, ½ cup of molasses, 2 teaspoonfuls of soda, 2 teaspoonfuls of salt. Bake 2½ hours in a slow oven. Can steam 1 hour and bake 1½.

Corn Bread.
Mrs. H. L. Hervey.

2 cups of corn meal, ½ cup flour, 1 cup sour milk, ½ cup melted butter, 1 tablespoonful of sugar, 3 eggs, beat the eggs and sugar till very light, then add the meal, flour, milk and butter. Stir well together, after which add ½ teaspoonful of soda dissolved in hot water. Stir well and bake quick.

Indian Bread.
Mrs. J. E. Allen.

6 cups sweet milk, 3 cups sour milk, 1 cup molasses, 7 cups meal, 3 cups flour heaped, 2 teaspoons soda; steam 1½ hours and bake 1 hour. This will make 2 loaves.

Indian Bread.
Mrs. E. J. Wilder.

4 cups of sweet milk, 3 of sour milk, 1 of molasses, 5 cups of meal, 3 of flour, soda to sweeten.

Johnny Cake.
Mrs. D. A. Prentice.

2 tablespoonfuls of melted butter, 1 egg, 2 cups of sweet milk, ½ cup of sugar or molasses, 2 teaspoonfuls baking powder, 2 cups each of corn meal and flour. Bake in a moderate oven.

Johnny Cake.
Mrs. M. E. Galpin.

1 cup sour milk, 2 eggs, 4 tablespoons flour, 2 tablespoons sugar, 1 teaspoon soda; thicken with meal and bake in a hot gem pan.

BREAKFAST CAKES.

Muffins.
Mrs. H. P. Wade.

One quart of flour, one pint of warm milk, one teaspoonful of salt, one-half gill of yeast; mix at night, and beat until very light. In the morning drop the dough in buttered rings; let stand twenty minutes, then bake.

Muffins.
Mrs. S. A. Northway.

One quart of milk, one-half pint of yeast, two well beaten eggs, a lump of butter one-half the size of an egg, and flour enough to make a stiff batter; let them stand until perfectly light, then bake on a griddle in the rings made for the purpose.

Breakfast Cakes.
Mrs. S. A. Northway.

Two-thirds of a cup of milk, two eggs beaten lightly, two cups of flour, one tablespoonful of meal, one tablespoonful of sugar, and butter the size of an egg, two teaspoonfuls of baking powder.

Muffins.

One quart of sour milk, two tablespoonfuls of butter, one of soda, and enough flour to make a thick batter.

Wheat Muffins.
Mrs. E. F. Mason.

One teaspoonful of melted butter, one egg, one and one-half cup of flour, one teaspoonful of cream tartar, one-half teaspoonful of soda, one-half cup of sweet milk; bake quickly in muffin pans.

Meal Muffins.
Mrs. E. F. Mason.

One and one-half cup of milk and water, one egg, one tablespoonful of sugar, a little salt, two heaping teaspoonfuls of baking powder, meal enough to make a thin batter.

Graham Gems.
Mrs. H. L. Hervey.

Two cups of Graham flour, one cup of sour milk, one tablespoonful of melted butter, one-half teaspoonful of soda dissolved into the milk (sweet milk and baking powder may be used if preferred). The gem tins should be well buttered and hot, and the gems baked quick.

Graham Gems.
Mrs. E. C. Wade.

One cup of buttermilk, one tablespoonful of butter, one-half teaspoonful of soda, a little salt, flour to make a stiff batter. Sweeten if you choose; bake in gem pans.

Breakfast Rolls.
Mrs. E. B. Leonard.

One pint of sweet milk, one or two eggs, a little salt, a little butter, three teaspoonfuls of baking powder. Stir the batter some thicker than you would for griddle cakes; bake quick.

Wheat Gems.
Mrs. T. Fricker.

To one cup of rich sour buttermilk add one teaspoonful of soda, a little salt, and flour enough to make a stiff batter; drop into hot gem irons and bake in a quick oven.

Oat Meal Breakfast Cakes.
Mrs. B. W. Baldwin.

One teacup of oat meal, one of sour milk; soak over night; one-half teacupful of molasses, one and one-half of wheat flour, one teaspoonful of soda, one teaspoonful of salt, two eggs.

Griddle Cakes.
Miss H. S. Kellogg.

One quart of thick sour milk, one quart of flour, five eggs, whites and yolks beaten separately, soda and a little salt.

Breakfast Corn Cakes.
Mrs. E. Latham.

One pint of not very sour milk, one egg, two tablespoonfuls of melted butter, one tablespoonful of sugar, two tablespoonfuls of flour, corn meal to make not very thick batter; bake in buttered gem tins.

Rice Croquetts.
Mrs. B. W. Baldwin.

Boil one cupful of rice till very soft; when cold, beat in two eggs, two teaspoonfuls of sugar, one of salt; form into pear shaped balls, dust a little flour over and roll them into two beaten eggs, and fry a little brown in boiling lard. Send to the table hot.

CRACKERS.

Mrs. N. E. French.

Seven cups of flour, one-half cup of water, one-half cup of butter, two teaspoonfuls of cream tartar, one teaspoonful of soda. One tablespoonful of cream improves them.

Cream Crackers.
Mrs. J. A. Howells.

One pint of cream, six eggs, the whites beaten separately. If the cream is sour, one teaspoonful of soda; add to the cream and eggs enough flour to make a stiff dough, a little salt; pound half an hour.

CAKES.

Cake Making.

To make a good cake one must be accurate in the proportions and should have fresh eggs, good sweet butter, and crushed sugar. It is also best to have an egg-beater, as you can beat the eggs much better in a very little time. Never beat your eggs or butter and sugar in a tin pan, as the coldness of the tin is apt to prevent them from becoming light, but always use an earthen or wooden vessel. On mixing, beat well together butter and sugar, beat separately the yolks and the whites of the eggs, then with the yolks, first stir the butter and sugar, next the flour and milk, if any is used, and lastly, the whites of the eggs and flavoring. If you desire to try your cake before baking, add about one-third of a teaspoonful of baking powder to a large spoonful of batter, then bake. It is not best to put baking powder into the cake and let it stand long before baking.

White Pound Cake.
Mrs. D. L. Crosby.

1 cup sugar, 1½ cups flour, ½ cup milk, ½ cup butter, 2 teaspoons baking powder, whites of 2 eggs.

Cup Cake.
Mrs. S. A. Northway.

Rub 3 cups sugar with 1½ cups butter; when white beat 3 eggs, and mix with butter and sugar together with 3 cups sifted flour, rose water and essence of lemon to taste. Dissolve 1 teaspoon soda in 1 cup sour milk, strain it into the cake, then add 3 cups more of sifted flour and 1 pound of seeded and chopped raisins.

Bridgeport Cake.
Mrs. Asaph Carter.

1 cup butter, 2 of sugar, 3½ of flour, 2 cups currants, 1 cup sour milk, 4 eggs, 1 teaspoon soda, juice and rind of 1 lemon.

One Egg Cake.
Mrs. M. Baldwin.

1 egg, ½ cup milk, 1½ cups flour, 1 cup sugar, 1 tablespoon melted butter, 1 teaspoon baking powder.

Ocean Cake.
Mrs. N. E. French.

2 cups powdered sugar, ½ cup butter, 1 of sweet milk, 3 of flour, 3 teaspoons baking powder, whites of 5 eggs.

Dover Cake.
Mrs. S. A. Northway.

1 cupful butter, 2 cupfuls sugar, 6 eggs, 1½ pints flour, 1 cup milk, 1 teaspoonful each royal baking powder, extract cinnamon and orange. Rub butter and sugar to a cream, add the eggs 2 at a time, beating 5 minutes, between each addition sift the flour and powder together. Bake in a ather hot oven 40 minutes.

Gold Cake.
Mrs. S. A. Northway

Yolks of 8 eggs, 2 cups sugar, 1 of butter, 1 of sweet milk, 4 of flour, 1 teaspoon soda, 2 of cream tartar, nutmeg.

Delicate Plum Cake.
Miss Fanny Dean.

1 cup sugar, 1 cup seeded raisins, 2 cups flour, ½ cup butter, ½ cup milk, 1 teaspoon cream tartar, ½ of soda, whites of 4 eggs, and flavor to taste.

Rochester Cake.
Mrs. B. F. Wade.

2 cups sugar, ⅔ cup butter, 3 of flour, 1 cup sweet milk, 3 eggs, 1 teaspoon cream tartar, ½ spoon soda. Put in 3 parts, baking two plain. To the third add 1 tablespoon molasses, 1 cup raisins chopped, ¼ cup citron, 1 teaspoon cinnamon, ½ cloves, 1 tablespoon flour. When done put together with jelly and frost the top.

Layer Cake.
Mrs. Allen Houghton.

Yolks of 2 eggs, 1 cup sugar, ⅔ cup sweet milk, 1 tablespoon melted butter, 1⅔ cups flour, 2 teaspoons baking powder. Bake in 3 layers and spread each with a cream or jelly. Use whites of eggs for frosting.

Roll Jelly Cake.
Mrs. B. F. Bowman' Sr.

3 eggs, 1 cup white sugar, 1 cup flour, 2 teaspoons cream tartar, 1 of soda.

Jelly Cake.
Mrs. Asaph Carter.

3 eggs, 1 cup sugar, 4 tablespoons sweet milk, 4 of melted butter, 1 teaspoon soda, 1 of cream tartar, 1½ cups flour.

CAKES.

Jelly Cake.
Mrs. M. Baldwin.

1 cup sugar, ¾ cup sweet milk, 1½ cups flour, 1 tablespoon butter, 1 egg, three teaspoons baking powder.

Apple Jelly Cake.
Miss H. S. Kellogg.

4 eggs, 1 cup sugar, butter size of an egg, 1 cup flour, 1 teaspoon cream tartar, ½ teaspoon soda. For the jelly—1 lemon, 1 cup sugar, 1 large sour apple grated, 1 egg. Beat together, and stir till they come to a hard boil. Make this first and set to cool.

Lemon Jelly Cake.
Mrs. E. C. Wade.

2 eggs, 2 cups sugar, not quite ½ cup butter, 1 cup sweet milk, 2½ flour, 1 teaspoon soda, 2 of cream tartar, 1 of lemon extract.

Jelly for above.

1 lemon, 1 egg, one-half cup water, one-half cup sugar, 1 tablespoon flour. Beat the egg and sugar, add the flour and grated rind and juice of the lemon, then stir into the boiling water. When cold spread between the layers of cake.

Lemon Roll Cake.
Mrs. S. W. Dickinson.

One cup sugar, three eggs, one tablespoon butter, 1 teaspoon baking powder, one cup flour. Stir ten minutes and bake in long tins.

Jelly for same.

One grated lemon, one cup sugar, one egg well beaten, one tablespoon water. Boil, and when nearly cool spread the cake with jelly and roll.

Lemon Cake.
Mrs. S. A. Northway.

Three cups sugar, one of butter, one of sour milk, five cups flour, five eggs, one teaspoon lemon extract, currants.

Sponge Cake.
Mrs. S. A. Northway.

Three eggs beaten together for five minutes, one and one-half cups powdered sugar added to the eggs and beaten five minutes longer, then add two cups flour, one-half cup boiling water last thing, one teaspoon cream tartar, one-half of soda, a little salt and lemon to taste.

Sponge Cake.
Mrs. D. L. Crosby.

Four eggs, two cups sugar, two cups flour, one-half cup cold water, two teaspoons baking powder. Makes two small loaves.

Sponge Cake.
Mrs. W. H. Ruggles.

One cup pulverized sugar, one-half cup flour, whites of five eggs, one teaspoon cream tartar.

Sponge Cake.
Mrs. Asa Bailey.

One cup sugar, one cup flour, four eggs. Beat sugar, whites and yolks together till very light. Add flour very lightly.

White Sponge Cake.
Miss M. Williams.

Whites of ten eggs, one goblet and one-half pulverized sugar, (common size) one goblet flour, one teaspoon cream tartar, beat eggs to stiff froth, sift cream tartar, flour and sugar together. Bake in moderate oven.

White Sponge Cake.
Mrs. S. W. Dickinson.

One cup of sugar, one and one-fourth cups of flour, whites of seven eggs, one teaspoon cream tartar, one-half teaspoon soda. Bake in jelly tins and spread with jelly or frosting.

Delicate Fruit Cake.
Mrs. Wm. Gibson.

Two and one-half teacups sugar, three and one-half cups sifted flour, one teacup butter, one of sour milk, one teaspoon soda, four eggs, flavor with lemon. Fill three jelly tins, to the remainder add one cup chopped raisins, one of currants, one-half of citron, two tablespoons molasses, one of cinnamon, one-half of cloves.

Ribbon Cake.
Mrs. Asaph Carter.

Two cups of sugar, one of butter, one of milk, four of flour, four eggs, one teaspoonful of cream tartar, one-half of soda. Fill two tins of equal size, one-third in each; to the remaining one-third add three teaspoonfuls of molasses, one teacupful of currants or raisins, chopped, a little cinnamon and spice to taste; place in layers when done, light and dark alternately, with jelly between; lay a piece of paper on top, turn on one of the tins and press with two flat-irons till cold.

CAKES.

Layer Cake.
Mrs. M. E. Galpin.

Light—Two cupfuls of sugar, two-thirds of a cupful of butter, one cupful of milk, three of flour, three eggs, two teaspoonfuls of baking powder.

Dark.—One-third of the batter, add to it one cupful of chopped raisins, one-third of a cupful of citron, one-third of a cupful of currants, one teaspoonful of cloves, two of cinnamon, one tablespoonful of flour; put together with jelly or frosting, dark layer in the center.

Cocoanut Cake.
Mrs. E. F. Abell.

Whites of three eggs, one cupful of sugar, one-half cupful of sweet milk, one and one-half of flour, two teaspoonfuls of baking powder, whites of two eggs for frosting; put on in layers with cocoanut sprinkled on.

Cocoanut Cake.
Miss Flora Lindsley.

One-half cupful of butter (scant), one and one-half of sugar, one-half cupful of corn starch, one-half cupful of sweet milk, two teaspoonfuls of baking powder, one and one-half cupfuls of flour, whites of six eggs.

Snowflake Cake.
Mrs. S. A. Northway.

Two cups of sugar, one cup of sweet milk, one-half cup of butter, four cups of flour, three eggs, one teaspoonful of cream tartar, one-half of soda; bake in layers, with thin icing between, sprinkled thickly with prepared cocoanut. Flavor as you like.

Chocolate Cake.
Miss Eliza Latham.

Two-thirds of a cup of butter, one cup of milk, two cups of sugar, three cups of flour, whites of eight eggs, three teaspoons of baking powder; bake in layers. Icing or jelly for same, one-half cake of chocolate, one cup sugar, one-half cup milk; boil together for jelly, or bake in loaf and use same for frosting.

Chocolate Cake.
Mrs. E. B. Leonard.

One cup butter, two cups sugar, three and one-half cups flour, one cup sweet milk, four eggs, two teaspoons baking powder.

Mixture.—Two squares bakers' chocolate grated, two cups

brown sugar, one-half cup sweet milk, white of one egg; boil till thick; flavor with vanilla.

Orange Cake.
Mrs. M. Baldwin.

Two cups sugar, one-half cup butter, one-half cup water, two cups flour, yolks of five and whites of four eggs beaten separately, one teaspoon soda, two of cream tartar, one orange grated, the white of one egg, and sufficient sugar to make it stiff placed between the layers.

Orange Cake.
Mrs. D. L. Crosby.

Two cups of sugar, two cups of flour, five eggs, reserving the whites of two for frosting, one-half cup cold water, two teaspoons baking powder, grated peel and juice of one orange; bake in layers; grated peel and juice of one orange in frosting.

Orange Cake.
Miss A. M. Lewis.

One-half cup butter, two of sugar, two and one-half of flour, two tablespoons sweet milk, one and one-half teaspoons baking powder, the yolks of five eggs, whites of three, grate outside and squeeze the juice of one orange into the cake, using another for icing; bake as jelly cake.

Mountain Cake.
Mrs W. H. Ruggles.

One pound sugar, one pound flour, one-half pound butter, one cup sweet milk, two teaspoons baking powder, six eggs, whites and yolks beaten separately; flavor with lemon.

Mountain Cake.
Mrs. J. E. Allen.

One cup sugar, one large cup flour, two eggs, or whites of four, one-fourth cup milk, one teaspoon cream tartar, one-half of soda; bake in two tins and put together with jelly.

Mountain Cake.
Mrs. S. A. Northway.

One pound butter, one pound sugar, one pound flour, one-half pound sour milk, one teaspoon soda, ten eggs, whites and yolks beaten separately; bake like jelly cake, with icing between.

CAKES.

Almond Cake.
Mrs. N. E. French.

One and one-half cups sugar, three-fourths cup butter, one-half cup milk, two cups flour, three eggs, two teaspoons baking powder, one-fourth pound blanched almonds.

Hickory Nut Cake.
Mrs. J. R. Fitch.

Two cups sugar, one cup sweet milk, three cups flour, one-half cup butter, two eggs, two heaping teaspoons baking powder, one pint each of meats, one cup raisins, one-half cup blanched almonds, all chopped.

Hickory Nut Cake.
Miss Minnie Dean.

One-half cup sugar, one-half cup butter, two cups flour, three-fourths cup sweet milk, one-half cup hickory-nut meats and one cup of seeded raisins, two eggs, one teaspoon cream tartar, one-half teaspoon soda.

Fig Cake.
Mrs. W. P. Howland.

Two cups sugar, one cup butter, one cup sweet milk, three cups flour, one teaspoon soda, two of cream tartar, whites of eight eggs; bake in layers. For filling, chop separately one pound raisins, three-fourths pound figs, and mix; then spread the cake with this, and then a layer of boiled frosting.

Fig Cake.
Mrs. N. E. French.

Two cups sugar, one-fourth cup butter, one cup sweet milk, two cups flour, one cup corn starch, whites of six eggs, one teaspoon baking powder; flavor with lemon.

DARK PART.

One cup sugar, one-half cup butter, one cup cold water, with teaspoon of soda dissolved in it, one and one-half cups chopped raisins, one-half pound figs, four eggs, cinnamon and cloves; bake in layers.

Blackberry Cake.
Mrs. W. P. Howland.

One cup sugar, three-fourths cup butter, one cup blackberry jam, one and one-half cups flour, three tablespoons sweet milk, one teaspoon soda, three eggs, cinnamon and nutmeg.

Marble Cake.
Mrs. E. B. Leonard.

Brown.—Yolks of four eggs, one cup brown sugar, one-half cup molasses, one-half cup butter, one-half cup sour milk, one-half teaspoon soda, one teaspoon cinnamon, one-half nutmeg, one-half teaspoon cloves, one-half teaspoon black pepper, one-half teaspoon allspice, two and one-half cups flour.

White.—Whites of four eggs, one-half cup sweet milk, one teaspoon cream tartar, one-half teaspoon soda, one cup white sugar, one of butter, two of flour.

Marble Cake.
Mrs. Alice E. Baldwin.

Light part.—One cup sugar, one-half cup each of butter and milk, whites of three eggs, two cups flour, one and one-half teaspoons baking powder.

Dark.—One-half cup brown sugar, one cup molasses, one-quarter cup each of butter and milk, two cups flour, yolks of three eggs, one and one-half teaspoons baking powder, three teaspoons of ground mixed spices. Put the batter into tin in alternate layers.

Mottled Cake.
Mrs. W. P. Howland.

Light part.—Two cups sugar, two-third cup butter, two and one-third cup sweet milk, three and one-half cups flour, one teaspoon soda, two of cream tartar, whites of eight eggs. Lemon flavoring.

Red part.—One cup sugar, one-third cup butter, one-third cup sweet milk, two cups flour, one teaspoon cream tartar, one-half teaspoon soda, whites of eight eggs. Vanilla flavoring. Color with rose syrup. Fill pan with spoonful of light, then with red until full.

Rose Syrup for above.

One-quarter oz. powdered alum, one quarter oz. cream tartar, one oz. powdered cochineal, four oz. loaf sugar, one saltspoon of soda. Boil ten minutes in a pint of water, when cool bottle tight.

Metropolitan Cake.
Mrs. J. R. Fitch.

White.—One and one-half cups white sugar, one-half of butter, one-half sweet milk, two and a half flour, whites of four eggs, two even teaspoons baking powder.

Dark.—One cup brown sugar, one-half molasses, one-half butter, one-half sweet milk, two and one-half flour, yolks of four eggs, two even teaspoons baking powder; add spices and fruit. Bake in layers, alternating light and dark. Frost each layer.

Watermelon Cake.
Mrs. Wm. Gibson.

White part.—Two cups sugar, one cup butter, one cup sweet milk, whites of eight eggs, three and one-half cups flour, two teaspoons cream tartar, one teaspoon soda.

Red part.—One cup red sugar, one-half cup butter, one-third cup sweet milk, two cups flour, whites of four eggs, one teaspoon cream tartar, one-half spoon soda, one cup seeded raisins. Place red part in the center.

Ice Cream Cake.
Mrs. Henry Wade.

One cup sugar, one-half cup butter, one-half cup milk, three eggs, two cups flour, two teaspoons baking powder. Bake in layers.

For Filling.

Whites of two eggs, four tablespoons sugar to one egg, one teaspoon of vanilla, a little more than a square of chocolate grated.

Buffalo Cream Cake.
Mrs. Wm. Gibson.

One egg, one cup sugar, one tablespoon butter, two-thirds cup milk, two teaspoons baking powder, one of vanilla, one and two-thirds cup flour; bake in three layers.

Cream for same.

One-half pint milk, one egg, one teaspoon corn starch, one tablespoon flour, two tablespoons sugar, vanilla. Scald the milk, beat sugar, flour, egg and corn starch together, and boil until it becomes thick. Add a little salt.

French Cream Cake.
Mrs. H. L. Hervey.

Three eggs, one cup sugar, one cup flour, two teaspoons baking powder, three tablespoons cold water, flavor to taste. Bake in jelly tins in three or four layers according to size of pans, and put between layers this second part: One cup sweet milk, one egg, one-half cup sugar, two teaspoons corn starch, piece of butter size of an egg. Place milk over fire, beat other ingredients together; when milk comes to a boil stir them in and boil till so thick it will not run from cake, when almost cold flavor with lemon, and when cold put together like any other layer cake. For a large cake take twice the amount called for.

Cream Puffs.
Mrs. B. F. Bowman, Jr.

One and one-half cups flour, two-thirds of a cup of butter, one-half pint of boiling water; boil water and butter together, stir in the flour while boiling; let it cool, then add five well-beaten eggs; drop in tins, and bake twenty minutes in a quick oven. When cold split open, and fill with cream.

Cream.

One pint of milk, one cup of sugar, two-thirds of a cup of flour, two eggs; beat eggs, sugar and flour together; stir this in the milk while it is boiling. When partly cool flavor with vanilla and nutmeg.

Cream Cake.
Mrs. J. E. Allen.

Two cups powdered sugar, three-quarter cup butter, one-half cup milk, three cups flour, four eggs, one teaspoon cream tartar, one-half teaspoon soda.

Cream for Same.

One-half cup sugar, one-half pint milk, one egg, two teaspoons corn starch, one teaspoon vanilla. Heat milk to boiling, stir in corn starch wet with cold milk, take out a little and mix with the well-beaten egg and sugar, then boil all together, stirring constantly until quite thick. Cool before seasoning, then spread on cake.

Cream Cake.
Miss H. S. Kellogg.

One cup boiling water, one heaping cup sifted flour, piece butter size of an egg. Scald together, then stir in four well-beaten eggs.

Custard for Filling.

To one quart of milk four eggs, sugar and flavoring to taste.

Election Cake.
Mrs. S. W. Dickinson.

One cup of yeast, one of sugar, one pint sweet milk, flour enough to make a stiff dough, and raise over night. Add one cup sugar, three quarters of butter, a little salt, allspice, cinnamon, raisins and currants, flour enough to stiffen;

raise again; when ready for oven rub a little milk and molasses over top, and when baked rub white of an egg over it.

"Old" Election Cake.
Mrs. B. F. Wade.

Four and one-quarter pounds flour, two pounds butter, three pounds sugar, three pints of milk, five eggs, one wine glass brandy one of wine, one nutmeg, fruit, raisins and citron.

French Loaf Cake.
Mrs. E. J. Wilder.

Two and one-half cups sugar, one and one-half cups butter, three eggs, yolks and whites beaten separately, one teaspoon soda, one and one-haf cups sour milk, one-half lb. raisins seeded, four cups flour. Makes two loaves.

Loaf Cake.
Miss Fannie Dean.

Two cups light bread dough, one cup sugar, one cup seeded raisins, slightly chopped, one-half cup butter, two tablespoonfuls sweet cream, one egg, one teaspoonful ground mace or nutmeg, one of cinnamon; mix together thoroughly with the hand, put into a buttered cake dish, and when it begins to rise, put into a slow oven.

Loaf Cake.
Mrs J. E. Allen.

Six cups light dough, one-fourth cup butter, three cups sugar, four eggs; when well mixed, add teaspoon cream tartar, one of soda, in a cup of thick cream; spice to taste.

Raised Cake.
Mrs. Allen Houghton.

Two cups sponge, one cup sugar, three-fourths cup butter. three eggs, one-half teaspoon soda, raisins and spices to suit taste.

Coffee Cake.
Mrs. Allen Houghton.

One and one-half cups sugar, one-half cup butter, two eggs, one-half cup strong coffee, one teaspoon saleratus dissolved in coffee, two cups flour, fruit if you prefer; bake in slow oven.

Coffee Cake.
Mrs. S. A. Northway.

One cup brown sugar, one cup molasses, one of butter, one of coffee, four of flour, one pound raisins, one pound currants, one teaspoon soda, one of cinnamon, one of cloves, one nutmeg; will keep six months.

Coffee Cake.
Mrs. H. L. Hervey.

One cup brown sugar, one cup molasses, three-fourths cup butter, one cup cold strong coffee, four cups flour, three eggs, two teaspoons soda dissolved in hot water, one nutmeg, one pound raisins, seeded, chopped and rolled in flour, will make two loaves.

Pork Cake.
Mrs. Asaph Carter.

One pound salt pork, one pint boiling water, four cups sugar, one cup molasses, one pound raisins, one pound currants, one-fourth pound citron, one teaspoon cinnamon, six cups flour, one teaspoon soda, one of cloves, one of nutmeg.

Pork Cake.
Mrs. Anna Albro, Buffalo, N. Y.

One pound fat salt pork chopped fine; turn over it two teacups boiling water, two cups New Orleans molasses, one cup brown sugar, seven of flour, one and one-half pounds raisins, one pound currants, two tablespoons each of cinnamon, cloves, allspice and nutmeg, one heaping teaspoon soda. This makes three large loaves, is equal to rich fruit cake, keeps a long time and improves with age.

Spiced Cake.
Miss S. Adele Crowell.

One cup sugar, one cup butter, one cup sour milk, three cups flour, one-half teaspoon each of cloves, nutmeg, cinnamon and soda, one cup seeded raisins.

Spice Cake.
Mrs. W. H. Ruggles.

One cup molasses, one of sugar, two-thirds cup butter, one cup sour milk, three eggs, one teaspoon soda, one nutmeg, one and one-half teaspoons cinnamon, one of cloves, three and one-half cups flour; two cups raisins are an improvement.

Spice Cake.
Miss Eliza Latham.

Two cups sugar, nearly one cup butter, three eggs, one cup sweet milk, three cups flour, one teaspoon soda, two of cream tartar; add chocolate with spices and raisins to darken it.

Angel's Food.
Mrs. M. H. King.

Take the whites of eleven eggs, one and one-half tumblerfuls granulated sugar, one of flour, one teaspoon of vanilla and one of cream tartar. Sift the flour four times, then add the cream tartar and sift again, but have the right measure before putting in the cream tartar. Sift the sugar and measure. Beat the eggs to a stiff froth on a large platter; on the same platter add the sugar lightly, then the flour very gently, then the vanilla. Do not stop beating until you put it in the pan to bake; bake forty minutes in a very moderate oven; try with a straw, and if too soft, let it remain a few minutes longer; turn the pan upside down to cool; when cold take out by loosening around the sides with a knife. Use a pan that has never been greased, and there must be on the edge three projections of tin an inch deep, so there will be a space between the pan and table when it is turned upside down. The tumbler for measuring must hold two and one-fourth gills.

Angel Food.
Mrs. Asa Bailey.

One tumbler flour, whites of ten eggs, one tumbler pulverized sugar, one teaspoon cream tartar.

White Cake.
Mrs. Lucien Gage.

One cup sugar, one-half cup butter, one cup sweet milk, two cups flour, one cup raisins, one-half spoon soda, one of cream tartar, whites of four eggs.

White Cake.
Mrs. M. Baldwin.

Whites of five eggs, one and one-half cup sugar, one-half cup milk, two cups flour, one-half cup butter, one and one-half teaspoons baking powder.

White Cake.
Miss Flora Lindsley.

Two cups sugar, whites of four eggs, five tablespoons butter, ten tablespoons sweet milk, two and one-half cups flour, two and one-half teaspoons baking powder.

White Cake.
Mrs. S. A. Northway.

Whites of twelve eggs beaten to a froth, one pound sugar, one pound flour, three-fourths pound butter, citron, one teaspoon lemon or vanilla and a little soda.

White Faced Cake.
Mrs. E. A. Sheldon.

Whites of four eggs, one and one-half cups sugar, one-third cup butter, two-thirds cup milk, two cups flour, two teaspoons baking powder.

Delicate Cake.
Mrs. E. J. Wilder.

Whites of four eggs, one cup sugar, one-half cup butter, one-half cup sweet milk, one teaspoon baking powder, one tablespoon corn starch, one and one-half cups flour.

Bride's Cake.
Mrs. M. Baldwin.

Whites of twelve eggs beaten to a stiff froth, two cups white sugar, one cup butter, two teaspoons cream tartar, one of soda, one cup sweet milk, five cups flour; put cream tartar in flour, soda in milk last of all.

Corn Starch Cake.
Mrs. Ralph Carter.

One and one-half cups sugar, one-half cup milk, one-half cup butter, one-half cup corn starch, one cup flour, whites of four eggs, two teaspoons baking powder.

Corn Starch Cake.
Mrs. W. H. Ruggles.

One cup butter, two of sugar, two of flour, one cup corn starch, one cup sweet milk, whites of five eggs, two teaspoon baking powder; flavor with lemon.

Snow-drift Cake.
Mrs. W. A. Van Duzer.

Three cups flour, two cups sugar, one-half cup butter, one cup sweet milk, whites of five eggs, two and one-half teaspoons baking powder.

Silver Cake.
Mrs. S. A. Northway.

Whites of eight eggs beaten to stiff froth, two cups sugar, one of butter, one of sour milk, four of flour, one teaspoon soda, two of cream tartar; flavor to taste.

White Fruit Cake.
Mrs. N. E. French.

One cup butter, two cups sugar, one cup sweet milk, two and one-half cups flour, whites of seven eggs, three teaspoons baking powder, one pound raisins, one pound figs, one pound dates, one pound almonds, one-fourth pound citron; blanch the almonds and cut fine.

CAKES.

Poor Man's Fruit Cake.
Mrs. Geo. Sheldon.

One cup chopped raisins, one cup sour milk, two cups syrup, one cup butter or drippings, two teaspoons soda, two handfuls dried apples soaked over night and chopped fine to make two teacupfuls; add one cup syrup and simmer till nearly dry; add fruit, cinnamon and spice to taste; stir quite thick.

Cheap Fruit Cake.
Mrs. C. C. Woodruff.

One cup each of butter, brown sugar, molasses and sweet milk, three cups flour, one pound each of raisins, currants, one teaspoon each of cloves, cinnamon, nutmegs and soda.

Fruit Cake.
Mrs. S. A. Northway.

One pound sugar, one pound butter, one pound flour, two pounds well washed currants, one-half pound citron, two pounds raisins, one-half of them seeded and all chopped, twelve eggs, whites and yolks beaten separately, one teaspoon soda, two of cinnamon, two of cloves, two of mace.

Excellent Fruit Cake.
Mrs. J. E. Allen.

One cup butter, one cup brown sugar, one cup molasses, one cup sweet milk, three cups of flour, four eggs, one and one-half teaspoon cream tartar, one of soda, two pounds chopped raisins, one nutmeg; will make two good loaves and keep moist six weeks.

Fruit Cake.
Mrs. J. A. Hervey.

Four cups light dough, three eggs, one cup butter, two of sugar, one nutmeg, two cups seeded raisins, added last; makes two loaves.

Fruit Cake.
Mrs. W. P. Howland.

Four pounds raisins, three pounds currants, one pound citron, one and one-half pounds sugar, one and one-fourth pounds butter, one and one-half pounds flour, one pound blanched almonds, three-fourth ounce cinnamon, one-fourth ounce cloves, one-half ounce allspice, three nutmegs, ten eggs.

Black Fruit Cake.
Mrs. B. F. Wade.

One pound flour, one pound sugar, three-fourths pound butter, three pounds raisins, two pounds currants, one pound citron, seven eggs, two cups sour cream, two cups molasses, two teaspoons cloves, two nutmegs, two teaspoons cinnamon, two of soda.

Dark Fruit Cake.
Mrs. B. W. Baldwin.

One pound brown sugar, three-fourths pound butter, one pound sifted flour, ten eggs, two pounds raisins, stoned and cut, two pounds currants well washed and dried, one-half pound citron cut in slips, one-half pound almonds blanched and cut, twelve figs cut in slips, one handful each of candied orange and lemon peel cut in slips, one wine glass rose water, one-half ounce mace, one-half nutmeg, one-half ounce cloves, one small teaspoon baking powder to each cup of flour.

Charlotte Russe Cake.
Miss Ada Simonds.

Six eggs, reserving whites of four, one and one-half cups sugar, one tablespoon butter, one-third cup milk, two cups flour, one heaping teaspoon baking powder; flavor to taste; bake in layers.

Custard for the above.

To one pint of milk add two tablespoons corn starch; when well cooked, take from the stove and add when cooled a little, the four whites, well beaten, stir well, sweeten and flavor.

Carolina Cake.
Mrs. H. L. Hervey.

Four eggs, two cups sugar, one cup sweet milk, four cups sifted flour, one-half cup butter, two teaspoons baking powder; flavor to taste. Very nice for layer cakes or baked in gem tins.

Carolina Cake.
Mrs. N. E. French.

One cup butter, two cups white sugar, four cups sifted flour, one cup milk, three teaspoons baking powder, whites of eight eggs.

Plaid Cake.
Mrs. N. E. French.

Cut ordinary fruit cake in small cubes; mix it through the above Carolina cake, and bake all together in a long tin and slice.

Vanity Cake.
Miss A. M. Lewis.

One-half cup butter, one cup sweet milk, three eggs, one and one-half cups sugar, two cups flour, two teaspoons baking powder; take out enough for one layer, add one cup of chopped raisins, one teaspoon cinnamon, one of nutmeg, one of allspice, and make this the center layer; put together with jelly or frosting.

Custard for Cake.—Cold.
Miss A. M. Lewis.

One-half cup sour cream, one cup sugar, yolk of one egg, beaten together; the whites of two eggs beaten separately, one-fourth pound almonds.

Same—Hot.

One cup sugar, two tablespoons corn starch, one egg, one pint sweet milk, a little butter; when almost cold add cocoanut and lemon flavoring.

Rose Custard for Cake.
Mrs. N. Z. Canfield, Buffalo.

Mix together one-fourth ounce powdered alum, one-fourth ounce cream tartar, one ounce powdered cochineal, four ounces loaf sugar, one-half teaspoon soda; boil ten minutes in one pint of hot water; when cold, bottle and cork tightly. One teaspoonful for a cake.

ICING FOR CAKE.

Boiled Frosting.
Mrs. Asa Bailey.

Four cups sugar, two-thirds cup boiling water; boil till it snaps; add whites of four well beaten eggs, and beat until cold.

Icing.
Mrs. Wm. Gibson.

Two and one-half cups sugar, one-half cup water; boil three minutes, and when cool add whites of three eggs slightly beaten; beat till cold, then spread.

Boiled Frosting.
Mrs. E. A. Sheldon.

Boil to soft wax one cup sugar in enough water to dissolve it; beat white of one egg and stir the sugar in slowly while hot; stir until cool and flavor.

Icing for Orange Cake.
Mrs. M. E. Galpin.

Beat whites of two eggs stiff, add juice and rind of one orange and thicken with sugar; spread between layers and on top.

Boiled Frosting.
Mrs. W. P. Howland.

Whites of three eggs beaten to a stiff frost, two cups granulated sugar, six tablespoons hot water; moisten sugar with water and boil without stirring till it ropes; pour upon the beaten egg and stir until cold.

COOKIES.

Cookies.
Mrs. E. F. Mason.

One-half cup butter, one cup sugar, half a teaspoon soda dissolved in one tablespoon of milk, two eggs; flavor with lemon; roll soft.

"Red Brook" Cookies.
Mrs. J. A. Hervey.

Ten spoonfuls sugar, two eggs, six spoonfuls melted butter, four spooufuls sour milk, one teaspoon soda; work soft and roll thin; bake in a quick oven.

Cookies.
Mrs. W. Gibson.

One cup sugar, one egg, one cup cream, half a teaspoon soda, a little salt.

Cookies.
Mrs. M. H. King.

One cup sugar, two-thirds cup butter, two tablespoons sweet milk, one egg, one teaspoon cream tartar, half a teaspoon soda; mix stiff, roll thin.

Cookies.
Mrs. W. H. Ruggles.

One and one-half cups sugar, half cup butter, one cup sweet cream, two eggs, one-half teaspoon soda; season with nutmeg; mix soft, roll out and bake in a quick oven.

Cookies.
Mrs. S. A. Northway.

One cup butter, two of sugar, half cup cream, or quarter cup sweet milk, three eggs, one teaspoon soda, two teaspoons cream tartar; flavor with nutmeg.

Water Cookies.
Mrs. B. F. Bowman' Sr.

One cup sugar, one cup shortening, one nutmeg, one teaspoon soda, two-thirds cup cold water.

Cookies.
Miss Flora Lindsley.

Two cups sugar, one cup butter, three eggs, one-quarter teaspoon soda.

Cookies.
Mrs. E. J. Wilder.

One egg, one cup butter, one cup sugar, three tablespoons milk.

Cream Cookies.
Mrs. B. C. Bowman, Jr.

Two cups sugar, one cup butter; stir to a cream; one cup milk, one egg; flavor with nutmeg; three tablespoons baking powder. Make the dough soft as possible, cut in squares, and dip in a plate of sugar; bake in a quick oven.

Seed Cakes.
Miss R. P. Dean.

One cup butter, one and one-half cups sugar, one cup milk, one teaspoon soda, one large spoonful caraway seed, two eggs; roll thin, cut out and bake in a quick oven.

Cookies.
Mrs. M. E. Galpin.

Two cups sugar, one cup butter, one cup sour cream, one lemon, juice and rind, two eggs, cream, butter and sugar; add cream with one small teaspoon of soda dissolved in it; the beaten egg and lemon mix as soft as possible. The lemon may be left out and nutmeg or other seasoning substituted.

Cookies without Eggs.
Mrs. S. A. Northway.

One cup cream, one-half cup butter, one and one-half cups sugar, one teaspoon soda, nutmeg.

Sugar Drops.
Mrs. E. C. Wade.

Stir to a cream three ounces of butter and six ounces of pounded sugar, then add three beaten eggs, one-half pound flour and half of a nutmeg. Drop this mixture in large spoonfuls on buttered plates, taking care to have them several inches apart; sprinkle small sugar plums on the tops and bake directly.

GINGER COOKIES.

Ginger Cookies.
Mrs. E. A. Sheldon.

One cup sugar. one of butter, one of molasses, one tablespoon ginger, one of cinnamon, two teaspoons saleratus dissolved in three tablespoonfuls of hot water; bake quick.

Ginger Cakes.
Mrs. W. H. Ruggles.

One cup New Orleans molasses, half cup lard, one tablespoon ginger, one large teaspoon soda; heat the molasses and lard together, put in your soda, pour into the flour and mix; cut with a knife into square cakes.

Molasses Cakes.
Mrs. E. J. Betts.

Two cups molasses, ten tablespoons water, eleven tablespoons butter, three tablespoons brown sugar, one tablespoon ginger, three teaspoons soda.

Ginger Drop Cakes.
Mrs. W. H. Ruggles.

One cup best New Orleans molasses, half cup butter, half cup water, three cups flour, two teaspoons of ginger, one teaspoon soda. Drop with a spoon on a buttered tin.

Ginger Drops.
Mrs. E. L. Lampson.

One-half cup lard, one cup brown sugar, one-half cup molasses, one cup sour milk, one teaspoon soda, two eggs, one teaspoon ginger; grease the dripping-pan well, make the batter so that it will drop from the spoon in drops not quite as large as an egg.

Graham Cookies.
Mrs. T. Fricker.

One cup sugar, one cup sour cream, teaspoon soda, little salt, one egg or none, and mix soft with sifted Graham flour.

Graham Cookies.
Mrs. W. P. Howland.

One coffee cup sugar, half teacup water, half teaspoon soda, butter size of an egg. Graham flour to mix soft.

Ginger Snaps.
Mrs. B. F. Bowman, Jr.

One-half cup butter, or pork drippings, one-half cup sugar, one cup molasses, one tablespoon ginger, one teaspoon saleratus, and flour enough to make them hard.

Ginger Snaps.
Mrs. B. W. Bowman.

Two cups New Orleans molasses, one cup lard and molasses scalded together, one teaspoon ginger, two teaspoons soda, one teaspoon salt, three tablespoons hot water.

Nice Ginger Snaps.
Mrs. N. E. French.

One pound sugar, one pint molasses, three-fourths pound butter, one cup sweet milk, two teaspoons saleratus, one tablespoon cinnamon, one tablespoon ginger; make stiff with flour, roll thin, bake quick.

Spiced Ginger Snaps.
Mrs. H. L. Hervey.

Two cups syrup, one and one-half cups sugar, half cup melted butter, three teaspoons ginger, two of cinnamon, two of allspice, two of cloves, two teaspoons soda dissolved in four tablespoons hot water; knead in flour till the dough is quite stiff, rub the tins each time they are filled with fresh lard, bake a light brown and remove from the tins as soon as taken from the oven; prick each one two or three times with a fork before putting in the oven.

Ginger Snaps.
Mrs. C. C. Woodruff.

One cup molasses, one cup sugar, one cup shortening, five large spoons boiling water, one teaspoon soda, one teaspoon ginger.

Lemon Snaps.
Mrs. E. B. Leonard.

One coffee cup sugar, a little more than half a cup butter, two eggs, two tablespoons hot water, half teaspoonful soda, flavor with lemon, roll thin.

GINGER BREAD.

Ginger Bread.
Mrs. D. A. Prentice.

One cup molasses, half cup sugar, three tablespoons cold shortening, three cups flour, two teaspoons soda, one cup boiling water poured over the whole; ginger and salt to taste; bake slowly; excellent with coffee.

Soft Ginger Bread.
Mrs. S. W. Dickinson.

One cup molasses, one-half cup butter, one-half sour milk, two eggs, one teaspoon ginger, one large teaspoon soda, flour to thicken.

Ginger Bread.
Mrs. M. E. Galpin.

One large cup molasses, one small cup sugar, small cup butter, one teaspoon soda dissolved in one cup boiling water, one and one-half tablespoons ginger.

Soft Ginger Bread.
Mrs. S. A. Northway.

One cup molasses, one cup butter, two of sugar, one cup milk, three of flour, four eggs, one tablespoon ginger, one-half of soda.

Ginger Bread.
Miss Ada Simonds.

One cup molasses filled with brown sugar, one cup sour cream, one teaspoon soda, one heaping teaspoon ginger, one egg, two and one-half cups flour. If you have no cream, a cup of buttermilk with three tablespoons of butter may be substituted; in this case use three cups of flour.

Ginger Cake.
Mrs. W. H. Ruggles.

One cup best New Orleans Molasses, one-half cup water, one-half cup butter, one teaspoon ginger, one-half teaspoon soda, two cups flour, one egg.

Soft Ginger Bread.
Mrs. E. B. Leonard.

One cup molasses, four tablespoons melted butter or lard, one heaping teaspoon soda in one-half cup of quite warm water, one tablespoon ginger. Do not stir too stiff, and bake in flat tins.

Old-fashioned Ginger Bread.
Mrs. S. A. Northway.

Two cups New Orleans molasses, one cup melted butter, two eggs, two even tablespoons soda, dissolved in hot water, one tablespoon ginger, a little salt and flour sufficient to roll out; bake in two square tins, mark with a knife one-half inch a part on top.

Another.—Good.
Mrs. S. A. Northway.

One pint molasses, one teacup melted butter, one-half teacup hot water with one teaspoon soda dissolved in it, two tablespoons ginger; the whole mixed thoroughly with enough flour to roll out and cut into cards; bake at once in quick oven.

Card Ginger Bread.
Mrs. T. Fricker.

One and one-half cups molasses (New Orleans), one-half cup butter and lard mixed, butter and molasses boiled together, two-thirds cup boiling water, one teaspoon soda, tablespoon ginger; mix soft as possible.

Soft Ginger Bread.
Mrs. T. Fricker.

One cup molasses, one cup sour cream, two and one-half cups flour, one egg, one teaspoon soda, one tablespoon ginger; bake in two tins.

Pop Overs.
Mrs. McCall.

One egg, beat very light, one cup sweet milk, one cup flour, a pinch of salt; bake in a quick oven in small cups.

Ginger Bread.
Miss Eliza Latham.

Two cups molasses, one cup water; stir with one cup of shortening; one even teaspoon alum dissolved in one-half pint of water, two large teaspoons soda, one spoon ginger, flour enough to make stiff; if lard is used add salt.

DOUGHNUTS.

Raised Doughnuts.
Mrs. E. C. Wade.

One large pint bread sponge, two cups sugar, one-half cup shortening melted in a pint of milk, two eggs, two teaspoons cinnamon, salt, mix moderately stiff.

Doughnuts.
Mrs. Henry Prentice.

One large cup butter, two cups sugar, one pint light sponge, four eggs, one pint milk, one teaspoon soda, a little nutmeg; let the dough rise twice.

Doughnuts.
Mrs. B. F. Wade.

One pint sweet milk, three eggs, one and one-half cups sugar, one nutmeg, five tablespoons melted butter, two and one-half quarts flour, mix well, three tablespoons baking powder.

Doughnuts.
Miss H. S. Kellogg.

Two cups sugar, two cups sweet milk, two eggs, piece of butter size of an egg, three teaspoons baking powder, flour enough to make a soft dough.

Quick Fried Cakes.
Mrs. E. C. Wade.

One-half pint buttermilk, three tablespoons butter, one egg, one cup sugar, one small teaspoon soda, cinnamon to flavor, flour to make a stiff dough; fry with moderate heat.

Fried Cakes.
Mrs. N. E. French.

One cup sugar, one tablespoon butter, one egg, three teaspoons baking powder, one cup sweet milk.

Fried Cakes.
Miss A. M. Williams.

Two cups sugar, one cup cream, two cups sour milk, two eggs, two nutmegs, two teaspoons soda, two of salt; mix soft.

Soda Fried Cakes without Eggs.
Mrs. E. F. Abell.

One pint sweet milk, two cups sugar, six tablespoons melted butter, two teaspoons soda, four teaspoons cream tartar; mix soft. If you like them shorter, add more butter.

Fried Cakes.
Mrs. S. A. Hervey.

One and one-half cups sugar, one and one-half cups sour milk (thick), three eggs, six spoons melted lard, one and one-half teaspoons soda, a little salt and cinnamon.

Fried Cakes.
Mrs. S. W. Dickinson.

One cup sugar, butter the size of an egg, two eggs, one cup sour milk, one teaspoon soda, a little salt and nutmeg, flour enough to knead well; fry in hot lard.

Fried Cakes.
Mrs. B. F. Bowman, Jr.

One quart flour, three teaspoons baking powder, three eggs, one cup sugar, butter the size of an egg; mix with water as soft as can be rolled.

CRULLERS.

Crullers.

One cup sugar, one cup sour milk, one egg, shortening the size of an egg, one teaspoon soda, nutmeg or cinnamon to the taste.

Crullers.
Mrs. E. F. Mason.

One cup sugar, one-half cup sweet milk, one tablespoons butter, two eggs, salt, one-quarter teaspoon saleratus.

Crullers.
Mrs. E. C. Wade.

For each egg take a tablespoon of melted butter, one heaping tablespoon of sugar, flavor with lemon, using grated rind and a little juice, mix stiff enough to roll well, cut in fancy shapes and fry quickly. It will be necessary to have all rolled and cut before you begin to fry, as they need constant attention.

Fritters.
Mrs. E. F. Mason.

One cup thick sour milk, one half teaspoon soda, one teaspoon salt, stir thick and drop with a spoon into hot lard.

Fritters.
Mrs. B. F. Wade.

One pint milk, three eggs, a little salt, one quart flour, one teaspoon bakingpowder, fry in hot lard.

PIES.

Pie Crust.

To one pint sifted flour add one even teaspoon baking powder and sweet cream enough to wet the flour, leaving crust a little stiff. This is sufficient for two pies.

Pie Crust.

One coffee cup lard, three of sifted flour, and a little salt. Cut it well into flour with a knife, then mix with cold water quickly, handling as little as possible; makes four pies. After rolling spread over butter and roll again, taking new slice of paste each time for top crust, the trimmings for under crust.

Graham Crust.

Mix lightly one-half pound Graham flour, one-half pint sweet cream, one-half teaspoon salt, roll and bake like other pastry.

Puff Paste.

To every pound of flour, add three-fourths of a pound of butter, the yoke of an egg; use ice cold water; chop half of the butter into the flour; then stir in the beaten yolk and as much water as needed; work all into a dough, roll out thin, spread on some of the butter, fold closely, butter side in, and re-roll; repeat this until the butter is all used up. Keep the paste in a cool place until you wish to make it into patties or pies.

Pie Crust.

One quart of flour, one-half pound lard, one-quarter pound butter, and with water knead until smooth; roll it out thin three times, touching it each time with the lard, sprinkling it with flour, and rolling it up to be rolled again.

Pie Crust Glaze.

To prevent the juice soaking through into the crust and making it soggy, wet the crust with a beaten egg just before you put in the pie mixture. If the top of the pie is wet with the egg it gives a beautiful brown.

Lemon Cream Pie.
Mrs. B W. Baldwin.

One lemon grated, two eggs, two tablespoonfuls flour, one cup sweet milk; mix the whole together, leaving out the whites for merangue; beat whites of eggs with four tablespoonfuls sugar to a stiff froth; place on top of pie when baked, and brown lightly in the oven.

Lemon Pie.
Mrs. E. B. Leonard.

Grate one lemon, mixing the juice with the grated rind, one cup water, one of sugar, yolks of two eggs, one teaspoonful butter, three tablespoons flour. Bake with only an under crust. When done beat the whites of two eggs with two tablespoons sugar, add a few drops of lemon and spread over the top; then return to the oven to brown lightly. This makes one pie and is very nice.

Lemon Pie.
Mrs. E. F. Mason.

One lemon, one cup sugar, one cup water, salt, one heaping tablespoonful corn starch.

Lemon Pie.
Mrs. D. L. Crosby.

Grated peel and juice of one lemon, two cups sugar, three eggs, reserving the whites of two for frosting, two tablespoons corn starch dissolved in cold water, two cups boiling water; cook in a covered dish in boiling water. This will cook while the crusts are baking; when done fill the crusts. Beat the whites to a stiff froth, add two tablespoons sugar, put on the top and set in the oven to brown.

Lemon Custard Pie.
Mrs. E. F. Mason.

One cup sugar, one cup water, one tablespoonful flour, three eggs, saving white of one for icing, two-thirds lemon, peel chopped fine, mix to a smooth paste.

Icing.—White of one egg, a little sugar; flavor; spread on the top after it is baked.

Lemon Pie.
Mr. S. A. Northway.

Three eggs, one cup sugar, one cup water, one grated lemon and a little butter. Baked in one crust.

Lemon Pie.
Mrs. T. Fricker.

One tablespoon corn starch wet up with cold water; pour cup of boiling water over it; add one cup sugar, juice and grated rind of one lemon, and last, one beaten egg. Bake with two crusts.

Another Lemon Pie.
Miss Fanny Dean.

Take a large lemon and remove the peel and seeds, put into a bowl and add one cup of sugar and half of the peel chopped very fine, press as for lemonade, take four tablespoons of flour, add a little water, make a smooth batter and pour on it while stirring half a pint of boiling water, add it to the lemon and sugar, add the yolks of four eggs and the white of one well beaten; line two common sized pie pans with paste, fill in the mixture and bake. Beat the three remaining whites with four tablespoons pulverized sugar and a little lemon extract to a stiff froth, spread it on the top of the pies, put them in the oven and brown lightly.

Lemon Pie.
Mrs. Lucien Gage.

One lemon, one cup raisins chopped fine; add two cups sugar, one-half cup molasses, one tablespoon corn starch, beat well together; add one cup boiling water. Dissolve corn starch in a little water.

Cream Pie.

Six eggs, two cups sugar, two teaspoonfuls cream tartar, one teaspoonful soda, dissolve in two teaspoonfuls cold milk, two cups sugar; rub the cream tartar in the flour and add the soda when it is ready to bake. This makes three pies. Split them when cold and put in this cream:

One pint milk, one-half cup sugar, one-half cup flour (or one tablespoonful corn starch), two eggs. Beat eggs, sugar and flour together and pour into the boiling milk; stir constantly over boiling water until thickened; flavor with lemon or vanilla.

Cream Pie.
Miss Ada Simonds.

One cup of sweet cream, two spoonfuls flour, three spoonfuls sugar; season with lemon.

Cream Pie.
Mrs E. J. Betts.

One cup milk, one teacup sugar, two tablespoonfuls corn starch, yolks of two eggs; let the milk boil, stir in the starch, then beat in the eggs and sugar. Bake the crust thin, put in the custard, and bake while preparing the meringue.

Meringue.—Beat the whites of two eggs to a stiff froth and add a little pulverized sugar: pour over the pie, then return to the oven to brown. Flavor custard to taste.

Custard Pie.
Miss Ada Simonds.

To one pint of milk add yolks of three eggs and white of one well beaten with two tablespoons of sugar; flavor with nutmeg or vanilla, and fill the crusts as usual; when baked cover immediately with meringue and set back in the oven a moment to brown lightly.

The meringue is made of the remaining whites beaten very lightly and sweetened with two desertspoonfuls of sugar.

Cream Currant Pie.
Mrs. T. Fricker.

One cup currants, one cup cream, one cup sugar, one tablespoon corn starch or one egg. Bake with two crusts.

New England Mince Pie.
Mrs. S. A. Northway.

Four pounds meat boiled and chopped, three pounds suet boiled and chopped, four pounds raisins stoned and chopped, one-half pound citron, five pounds sugar, one quart molasses, one quart boiled cider, eight pounds crackers; mix cider and molasses together, add to the mixture five teaspoons ground cloves and ten of ground cinnamon, five of ground mace, one of black pepper, and six tablespoons of salt. Mix all the ingredients thoroughly together, and when making the pies, add bits of butter and a few whole raisins, and grate nutmeg on each.

Summer Mince Pie.
Mrs. Asa Bailey.

One and two-thirds cups crackers rolled fine, one cup raisins chopped fine, one cup whole raisins, one cup sugar, one cup molasses, two cups hot water, one-half cup butter, two-thirds cup vinegar, two teaspoons cinnamon, one teaspoon cloves; makes three pies.

Mince Pie.
Mrs. H. L. Hervey.

Two and one-half bowls meat, five bowls chopped apples, one pound raisins, one pound currants, one pint syrup, three cups sugar, one cup vinegar, one tablespoon lemon extract, add water till thin enough to bake. If you have boiled cider, use in place of vinegar and water.

Mock Mince Pie.
Mrs. W. P. Howland.

One cup molasses, one cup vinegar (not too strong), one cup sugar, one cup raisins, one cup bread-crumbs, one tablespoon cloves, one tablespoon cinnamon, one nutmeg, butter size of a butternut.

Apple or Peach Meringue Pie.

Stew the apples or peaches, and sweeten to taste. Mash smooth and season with nutmeg. Fill the crusts and bake until just done. Put on no top crust.

Take the whites of three eggs for each pie and whip to a stiff froth, and sweeten with three tablespoonfuls powdered sugar. Flavor with rose water or vanilla; beat until it will stand alone, then spread it on the pie one-half to one inch thick, and set back into the oven until the meringue is well "set." Eat cold.

Dried Peach Pie.
Miss Fannie Dean.

Soak the peaches over night; in the morning stew soft; make them quite juicy; slice into these one-third as much green pieplant as there is of the peaches; make the paste in the usual manner, and when the fruit is filled into the under crust, dredge it well with flour, cover and bake. This makes a better pie than either the peaches or pieplant alone.

Pumpkin Pie.
Mrs. S. A. Northway.

One pint stewed pumpkin, four eggs, one quart milk, one large cup sugar, one-half tablespoon ginger, grate a little nutmeg over the pie when ready to put in the oven. This will make two pies.

Pumpkin Pie.
Mrs. B. F. Wade.

One quart pumpkin, one quart milk, two cups sugar, four eggs, one tablespoon cinnamon, one teaspoon ginger, one nutmeg.

German Pie.
Mrs. E. F. Mason.

Under crust.—A little sifted flour, apples, sliced quite thick, butter, sugar, tablespoon water, nutmeg or cinnamon; bake the last few minutes with a tin over the top.

Silver Pie.
Mrs. E. F. Abell.

One large potato peeled and grated, the juice and grated rind of a lemon, the whites of two eggs well beaten, one cup water; beat well together and bake with one crust. When done, beat the whites of two or three eggs to a stiff froth with nearly one-half cup of fine sugar; set in the oven to brown lightly. Be sure and not grate the potatoes till you want to use them, as they turn black.

Shells for Tarts.

Cut with biscuit cutter nice puff paste, then with a wine glass or smaller cutter, cut out center of two out of three of these; lay the rings thus made on the third and bake at once; filled with jelly and covered with a meringue made of tablespoon of sugar to white of one egg, then browned in oven.

Almond Tarts.

Three eggs, one-fourth pound sugar beaten to a cream; add one-half pound shelled almonds pounded slightly; bake eight minutes.

Apple Pie.

Pare, core and slice ripe, tart apples; line your dish with a good crust and fill with the sliced apples; cover lightly with crust and bake. When it is done, slip a knife under the edge of the upper crust and remove it. Sweeten the apple to taste, stir in a teaspoonful of butter and season with nutmeg, then replace the crust.

Rhubarb Pie.

Skin the stalks with care, cut into small pieces; pour boiling water over the pieces and let it stand till you are ready to use. Having prepared your crust, fill it with the scalded fruit; over this grate the rind of one lemon and add a very little of the lemon juice; add one teacup sugar for a pie of the common size tins, and strew generously with flour; cover with a crust, fastening it carefully at the edges, and bake.

PUDDINGS.

In boiling pudding, have plenty of water in the pot boiling when the pudding is put in, and do not let it stop; add more as it is needed. Turn the pudding frequently. If a cloth is used, dip the pudding (when done) into a pan of cold water, so that it can be removed easily.

In using molds, grease well with butter, tie the lid closely, and set in a pot with very little water, and add more as needed.

Fruit sauces are nice for blanc-mange and corn starch puddings.

Fresh red cherries, stewed, sweetened and passed through a sieve, and slightly thickened with corn starch, make a good sauce.

Cottage Pudding.
Miss H. S. Kellogg.

One quart milk, one pint sifted flour, five eggs, whites and yolks beaten separately, the whites stirred in just before going into the oven. Bake one hour. Serve with sauce.

Cottage Pudding.
Mrs. Asa Bailey.

One pint flour, one cup sugar, one egg, piece of butter size of an egg, one cup sweet milk, three teaspoonfuls baking powder. Mix like cake; bake and serve while warm with liquid sauce.

Congress Pudding.
Mrs. S. A. Northway.

One cup butter, one cup sugar, one pint bread crumbs; boil one quart milk and pour over the above: mix well together, add the beaten yolks of four eggs, and bake three-quarters of an hour. When baked spread jelly over the top, and over that the whites of four eggs beaten with four tablespoonfuls of sugar. Set in the oven to brown.

Apple Dumplings.

Take tart, mellow apples, pared, remove the core and fill the place with sugar; then take one quart of flour, two or three teaspoonfuls of baking powder, and one-half tablespoonful of shortening; mix with sweet milk or water—

mix soft as possible—and roll it out; cut in squares of sufficient size to roll the apples in, set on plate and place in steamer.

Apple Shortcake.

To one quart of sifted flour add two small teaspoonfuls of cream of tartar, half a teaspoonful of salt; mix it with sweet milk in which one small teaspoonful of soda has been mixed, after dissolving in water. Roll out the dough, and put a teacupful of butter on it in small bits, and roll them in thoroughly. Bake the dough in two pieces. Split open each cake, spread with butter quickly, and cover with apple jam, or any kind of apple sauce. Pour some sweet cream over the top of the apple, grate nutmeg over it, and cover with the other half, placed crust side down; spread it with butter, and proceed as before. You can make this shortcake of one layer of apple jam, or one with three layers. It makes a delicious dessert dish, and a good relish for the tea table.

Southern Rice Pudding.

One quart fresh milk, one cup raw rice, two tablespoonfuls butter, one cup of sugar, four eggs, beaten light, grated peel of half a lemon, pinch of cinnamon and the same of mace. Soak the rice in the milk for two hours in a farina-kettle, surrounded by warm water. Then increase the heat, and simmer until the rice is tender. Cream, butter and sugar, and whisk into the eggs, until very light. When the rice is almost cold, stir all together, and bake in a buttered dish three-quarters of an hour. Eat warm with sauce, or cold with sugar and cream.

Rice Pudding.
Mrs. B. W. Baldwin.

Boil one-half cup of rice and one cup of raisins in one qt. of milk until soft; beat yolks of four eggs with six tablespoonfuls of sugar into the hot milk and rice *after* it is taken from the fire. Pour into a pudding dish and spread over the top a meringue made of the four whites beaten stiff with four tablespoonfuls of sugar, and flavored with vanilla or lemon. To be eaten cold.

Lemon Rice Pudding.
Miss E. Latham.

Boil one cup rice in one pint of water until dry: add one quart milk; boil until thick. Then add the yolks of three eggs beaten with six tablespoons sugar and rind of one lemon. Mix well and turn into a pudding dish. Beat the whites to a froth, add six tablespoons sugar, juice of one lemon, and spread over pudding. Brown in the oven.

Rice Pudding.
Mrs. E. C. Wade.

One teacup rice, one quart milk, one-half cup sugar, three eggs, a little salt. Put the rice on the stove with the milk and let it cook slowly till nearly dry. Then add the yolks of the eggs well beaten with the sugar. Beat the whites stiff, add a spoonful of sugar: spread it over the top and set in the oven to brown. Serve warm with jelly.

English Pudding.
Mrs. E. F. Mason.

Three cups sweet milk, one cup molasses, five cups flour, two cups seeded raisins, three teaspoons soda dissolved in water, two teaspoons melted butter, two teaspoons cinnamon, a little cloves and salt. Boil three hours in a pail set in water.

English Plum Pudding.
Mrs. J. A. Howells.

One pound plums, one pound raisins, one pound beef suet, one ounce citron, one ounce orange peel, one ounce candied lemon, six ounces flour, four ounces bread crumbs, eight eggs, and a little milk; steam four hours.

Fig Pudding.

Take half a pound of the best figs, wash them and chop them fine, two teacups grated bread (crusts for one may be used), one-half cup sweet cream, one cup sweet milk, one-half cup sugar; mix the bread-crumbs with the cream, then stir in the figs, then the sugar and the last thing get in the milk; pour into a mold or a pudding-dish and steam for three hours.

Steamed Pudding.
Mrs. S. A. Northway.

Three eggs, well beaten, two tablespoons sugar, two tablespoons butter, three-fourths cup sweet milk, one cup chopped raisins, two cups flour; steam one and one-fourth hours.

Steamed Pudding.
Mrs. S. A. Northway.

One quart flour, two cups sweet milk, one cup suet chopped fine, one-half cup sugar, one-half cup molasses, a little salt. Mix and put in a basin closely covered; place in a steamer and cook three hours.

Steamed Pudding.
Mrs. B. W. Baldwin.

Two cups sour milk, one and one-half cup Indian meal, two cups wheat flour, one-half cup chopped raisins, one teaspoon soda, a little salt. Eat with sweetened cream.

Steamed Blackberry Pudding.

One quart berries, one and one-fourth pounds flour, two gills beef suet, two gills molasses, two gills milk, two gills brown sugar, one teaspoon soda dissolved in one teaspoon boiling water. Mix the sugar, molasses, suet and milk together, then add flour and fruit alternately; butter the mould before putting the pudding in and steam three hours. To be eaten with hard sauce. It may be steamed in a two quart basin. It is good the next day sliced and fried.

Lemon Pudding.

Beat the yolks of two eggs light, add two cups sugar, dissolve four tablespoons corn starch in a little cold water, stir into two teacups boiling water, put in juice of two lemons with a little grated peel; mix all together with one teaspoon butter and bake fifteen minutes; when done, spread over the top the beaten whites and brown in oven.

Tapioca Pudding.
Mrs. E. F. Mason.

Three tablespoons tapioca soaked eight hours, one pint milk, two eggs (save the white of one to put over the pudding), sweeten to taste, raisins, salt and lemon; bake three-fourths of an hour.

Tapioca Pudding.
Mrs. S. A. Northway.

Eight tablespoons tapioca soaked in water three hours, five eggs, one quart milk, two tablespoons butter and a little nutmeg; bake three-fourths of an hour.

Tapioca Pudding.
Mrs. S. A. Northway.

Three tablespoons tapioca soaked until soft, one quart milk, put in a double kettle or a pitcher set in boiling water; when the tapioca is sufficiently tender, add the beaten yolks of three eggs, a small teacup of sugar, and a little salt. Stir this into the boiling milk, season with vanilla; pour one-half into a dish, then add the whites of the eggs beaten to a froth; pour the remainder on top. Eaten cold, it is very nice.

Tapioca and Apple.
Mrs. S. A. Northway.

Pare and core one dozen large apples (taking care not to break the apples); fill the hole with sugar, a very little butter and cinnamon; pour over them a preparation of one-half cup tapioca soaked in water over night, in one pint of water. Bake three-fourths of an hour; serve with sugar and cream.

Peach Tapioca.
Mrs. E. F. Mason.

Soak a teacupful of tapioca until soft, then add alternately in a deep dish, tapioca, peaches and sugar, a little butter and a sprinkle of salt. Fresh or canned peaches may be used; if fresh ones, pour a half cup of water over the top; if canned ones, use the juice: it is richer. The whites of three eggs beaten and browned on the top are an improvement.

Baked Indian Pudding.
Mrs. S. A. Northway.

One quart milk, four eggs, five tablespoons corn meal, one-half teacup sugar, and a little nutmeg. Boil the milk and scald the meal in it. Let it cool before you add the eggs. Bake three-quarters of an hour.

Old-Fashioned Indian Pudding.
Mrs. S. A. Northway.

Boil one quart sweet milk, stir in gradually seven tablespoons corn meal, add one pint molasses, one teaspoon cinnamon, and one quart cold milk; stir thoroughly; butter the dish in which it is to be baked, and bake two hours.

Baked Indian Pudding.
Mrs. J. E. Allen.

Scald one quart milk, add seven tablespoons corn meal while hot; when cool, add one-half cup sugar, one egg, one teaspoon salt, ginger or cinnamon.

Batter Pudding.
Mrs. S. W. Dickinson.

One quart milk, eight eggs beaten very light, eight tablespoons flour, a little salt. Bake and serve immediately with liquid sauce.

Ginger Pudding.
Mrs. E. A. Sheldon.

One egg, one cup molasses, one-half cup fruit, one-half cup hot water, one tablespoon ginger, one teaspoon soda; stir stiff and steam one hour.

Roly-Poly Pudding.
Mrs. E. C. Wade.

Make a light paste as for pie crust, or better still, as for short-cake, roll out, spread with fruit, either fresh or preserved; roll up, fastening ends tightly; steam or bake; eat with cream and sugar, or any liquid sauce.

Sour Cream Pudding.
Mrs. B. F. Wade.

One pint flour, one pint sour cream, one pint milk, six eggs, well beaten, add cream with just enough soda to sweeten, the last thing before baking; bake one-half hour.

Paste Pudding.
Mrs. C. S. Simonds.

Six tablespoons flour, six tablespoons sugar, six eggs, mix flour with milk like starch, then pour on a quart of boiling milk. Let it cool before adding the rest; bake half an hour, eat with hard sauce.

Paste Pudding.

This pudding is very good mixed like the one above, but made with six spoons flour, four spoons sugar, four eggs, one quart milk.

Apple Pudding.
Mrs. D. C. Lewis, Mt. Vernon.

Peel and quarter six good-sized apples and put in a dish with a little water, one pint of flour with one heaping teaspoonful baking powder well stirred through the flour, one egg, and one teacup of sweet milk; stir to a batter and pour over the apples. Set the dish on the stove, tightly covered for twenty minutes, loosen with a knife at the edge, and place a plate on it and turn bottom upward on the plate. Eat with sugar and cream.

Snow Pudding.
Mrs. H. P. Wade.

One-half box Cox's gelatine, pour over it one-half pint of cold water, and let stand one hour; then pour over it one-half pint of boiling water, one-half pound of sugar, juice of two lemons. Let cool, and when like thin jelly or boiled custard, take whites of three eggs beaten stiff and mix thoroughly, then turn into moulds.

Spanish Cream.
Mrs. H. P. Wade.

One-half box Cox's gelatine, one small cup of sugar, yolks of three eggs, one quart of milk. Soak gelatine in milk one hour, then put it over the fire and let scald, then stir in eggs and sugar after being well beaten, and let come to a boiling point, but *not* boil. Flavor with vanilla and pour into moulds.

Orange Pudding.
Mrs. B. W. Baldwin.

Pare and slice six oranges and lay in pudding dish; sprinkle nearly one cup of sugar over them.

Make boiled custard of one quart of milk, one cupful of sugar, yolks of three eggs, and two tablespoonfuls corn starch. When nearly cool, pour over the oranges; Beat whites to a stiff froth, spread on plate and brown slightly in the oven; then carefully spread over pudding.

Black Pudding.
Mrs. B. W. Baldwin.

One cup molasses, one cup sweet milk, one-half cup butter, two and one-half cups flour, one cup raisins, one teaspoon each of soda, cinnamon and allspice. Steam two hours. Eat with cream and sugar or maple syrup.

Corn Starch Pudding.
Mrs. Alice Baldwin.

Boil one quart of milk, then beat the yolks of four eggs with four tablespoonfuls of corn starch and a little milk; stir into the boiling milk, let it boil up once, and turn into a pudding dish; then beat the whites of the eggs to a froth and add four spoonfuls of powdered sugar; cover the pudding with the mixture, and set in the oven and brown lightly. Flavor with vanilla or lemon; the frosting is improved by adding a flavor to it.

Suet Pudding.
Mrs. B. W. Baldwin.

One cup sugar, one cup chopped suet, one cup water, three cups flour, one teaspoonful ginger, teaspoonful soda, one teaspoonful salt, one cup chopped raising; steam two hours in two quart basin. Eat with jelly sauce.

Rich Suet Pudding.
Mrs. B. W. Baldwin.

One and one-half cups zante currants, one cup raisins, one cup brown sugar, one cup flour, one cup suet—chopped fine—one cup cider, yolks of three eggs, one and one-half teaspoons soda. Steam three hours in two quart basin with cloth tightly tied over the top.

PUDDINGS.

Suet Pudding.
Mrs. C. S. Simonds.

One cup suet, chopped fine, one cup raisins chopped, one cup molasses, one cup sour milk, one teaspoon soda, three and one-half cups flour. Steam three hours.

Suet Pudding.
Mrs. S. A. Northway, and Mrs. E. F. Mason.

One cup suet chopped fine, one cup molasses, one cup sweet milk, four cups flour, one cup raisins (not chopped,) one teaspoon cinnamon, one teaspoon soda, one teaspoon salt. Steam in a pudding dish or boil in a bag three hours, or steam two and one-half hours, then bake one-half hour.

Suet Pudding.
Mrs. H. P. Wade.

One teacup of suet, one and one-half cups of raisins chopped, two teacups of sugar, one and one-half of milk, teaspoon salt, and one of soda. Make as thick as cup cake, and boil three hours.

Bread Pudding.
Mrs. E. F. Abell.

One quart milk, one cup sugar, one pint bread-crumbs, three eggs (saving the white of one to use for the top when baked). Cranberries on the top under the meringue are nice.

Steamboat Pudding.
Mrs. E. L. Lampson.

One cup sugar, one-half cup butter, one and one-half cups flour, four eggs, two teaspoons baking powder, raisins and currants if you wish. Steam three-quarters of an hour; eat with liquid sauce.

Cake Pudding.
Mrs. C. S. Simonds.

Three tablespoons melted butter, mix while warm with one cup powdered sugar, one pint sifted flour, one cup sweet milk, one egg, two teaspoons cream tartar, one teaspoon soda; beat hard and bake twenty minutes in a small oval or round dish. Eat with liquid sauce.

Bird's Nest Pudding.
Miss R. P. Dean.

Pare and core eight or ten pleasant apples, leaving them whole. Make a batter of one cup buttermilk, one-half teaspoon soda, a little salt, one egg, and flour enough to make it stiff. Place the apples in a pudding dish, pour the batter over them and steam one hour. Serve with sweet sauce or cream and sugar.

Baked Blackberry Pudding.
Mrs. Rockafeller.

One-fourth pound butter, one pound brown sugar, six ounces flour, four eggs, one quart blackberries, cream the butter, add the sugar gradually, then the yolks of the eggs; beat until very light, beat the whites to a stiff froth, add them alternately to the flour; stir the blackberries very gently into the batter, pour it into a buttered pudding-dish, and bake an hour. To be eaten hot, with wine sauce or fairy butter.

Whortleberry Pudding.
Mrs. E. F. Abell.

One pint molasses, one teaspoon soda well beaten into the Molasses, add a little salt, one teaspoon of ground cinnamon, one teaspoon of cloves, three pints of berries and flour to make a stiff batter; boil three hours. Serve with sauce.

PUDDING SAUCE.

Pudding Sauce No. 1.
Mrs. S. A. Northway.

One cup sugar, one cup water, one-half cup butter, one tablespoon flour; boil and flavor to taste.

Pudding Sauce No. 2.
Mrs. S. A. Northway.

Two eggs well beaten, one cup sugar, one cup butter (one-half will do), one and one-half cups boiling water; scald, but do not boil; flavor to taste, two tablespoons cider vinegar, or juice of a lemon.

Pudding Sauce No. 3.
Mrs. S. A. Northway.

Beat one cup sugar, one-half cup butter, with enough nutmeg to flavor, and six eggs. Then make a very thin gravy with one and one-half cups hot water; when this has boiled sufficiently, strain it on the other ingredients and whip it well. You can use an acid if you like.

Sauce for Ginger Pudding.
Mrs. E. A. Sheldon.

One egg, one cup sugar, one-third cup butter, one tablespoon flour, one and one-half tablespoons lemon; pour boiling water over it until it is like thin starch.

Hard Sauce.
Mrs. E. C. Wade.

Stir to a cream one and one-half cups sugar and one-half cup butter, smooth into a good form and grate nutmeg over the top.

Or, if you prefer, you can beat in the juice of a lemon and color with the rind. It may be colored with chocolate when that flavor is desirable. It will be more ornamental colored with cherry, currant or cranberry juice and arranged in alternate lines of pink and white.

Pudding Sauce.
Mrs. S. W. Dickinson.

One and one-half cups light brown sugar, one tablespoon corn starch, one tablespoon butter, two tablespoons vinegar or juice of one lemon, two cups boiling water. Mix starch, sugar and butter well together, pour boiling water over and boil five minutes.

Pudding Sauce.
Mrs. B. W. Baldwin.

Stir to a cream one cup of sugar and one-third cup of butter, beat in the yolk of one egg, flavor; then pour on one-half cup of hot but not scalded milk; beat the white of one egg to a stiff froth and stir in lightly.

Foam Sauce.

One teacup white sugar, piece of butter size of an egg, beat together with one egg until it foams; add one tablespoon vinegar. Just before serving stir in a thin batter made with one teacup boiling water and a spoonful of flour. You can use any flavoring you choose in place of the wine.

Sauce.

Beat whites of three eggs to a stiff froth, stir in three tablespoons of sugar; make sauce just as you are to use it, not as good to stand. Flavor to taste; a little vinegar improves it.

Sauce.

Take yolks of three eggs, one pint of milk, make a custard or sauce of cream and sugar, flavor with lemon.

AMBROSIA, CUSTARDS, &c.

Ambrosia.
Mrs. S. A. Northway.

One package of desicated cocoanut, six lemons and six oranges; pare and slice the lemons and oranges; put a layer of fine sugar in a dish, then a layer of lemons, a layer of cocoanut, then a layer of orange, then cocoanut and so on until the dish is filled; put sugar between each layer.

Ambrosia.
Mrs. H. L. Hervey.

Two cocoanuts, two pine-apples, six oranges; pare and slice very thin the pine-apples and oranges; grate the cocoanuts; put a layer of fine sugar in the bottom of the dish, then one of cocoanut, then orange and more sugar and cocoanut; next pine-apple, and so on till all is used, finishing with cocoanut and sugar. This is very nice for tea or evening company, and is best prepared several hours before using.

Boiling Rice.
Mrs. S. A. Northway.

Wash in three or four waters, removing all imperfect grains; to one pint of rice put three pints of boiling water and a little salt; let it boil seventeen minutes from the time it begins; remove the lid and put it on the back of the range to dry out, thus securing the grains white, separate and dry.

Angel's Food.
Mrs. S. A. Northway.

Make a rich custard, pour some in a glass dish; put a a layer of sliced cake on it; stir some finely powdered sugar into quince or currant jelly and spread over the layer of cake; pour on more custard, then another layer of cake and icing.

Floating Island.
Mrs. B. W. Baldwin.

One quart of sweet milk, sweeten to taste; when boiling add one and one-half tablespoonfuls of corn starch dissolved in a little cold milk; stir three minutes; remove from the fire, add the beaten yolks of five eggs, stirring briskly; must be very smooth and soft; flavor with one teaspoonful of vanilla; set aside to cool; just before serving heat the whites of five eggs very stiff with three-fourths of a cup of currant and raspberry jelly (one-half of each). Serve the ice cold custard in saucers and drop a large tablespoonful of the pink froth on each.

Custard.
Mrs. E. F. Mason.

One cup of milk for each person, heat until it boils, yolk of one egg for each cup of milk, cup of sugar to six cups of milk, three tablespoonfuls of corn starch to six cups, lemon and pinch of salt; beat this and add when milk is boiling, boil two or three minutes, beat the whites of two eggs to a froth, add lemon and sugar to taste; spread over the top. To be eaten cold.

Blanc-Mange.
Mrs. H. P. Wade.

Season one quart of cream or rich milk with five ounces of sugar and a few drops of vanilla, whip to a stiff froth; after soaking one ounce of gelatine in one pint of cold water for one hour, let it simmer until perfectly dissolved, stirring often; when lukewarm, pour the cream in and stir all the time till stiff enough to drop from a spoon, then pour into wet moulds.

Croustades with Stewed Fruit.
Mary Hooper.

Take a French roll a day old, cut off the crust, divide it into three equal portions; with a sharp knife cut out the middle of each, so as to form a basket; the sides of the croustades should be about the third of an inch thick; have a stew-pan half full of fat, and which is hot enough to color the bread instantly, immerse the croustades in it, and in less than half a minute they will be done; it is best to fry one or two at a time; take them out of the fat with a wire spoon or a skimmer, and dry them on paper; now fill the croustades with stewed fruit of any kind, and serve immediately after filling.

Apple Snow.
Mrs. S. A. Northway.

Pare and core one dozen large apples; put them in cold water and stew until soft; pulp through a sieve and sweeten to taste with white sugar. Put in a glass dish, beat the whites of twelve eggs to a froth with one-half pound of pulverized sugar; flavor with lemon or vanilla. Pile this on the apple very high. A pretty dish for tea.

Iced Apples.
Mrs. S. A. Northway.

Pare and core one dozen large apples (punch out the core, taking pains not to break the apple,); fill with sugar, very little butter and cinnamon; bake until nearly done; let them cool, and if you can without breaking, put on another dish, prepare some icing, lay on top and sides, and set into the oven to brown slightly. Serve with cream.

Fried Cream.
Mrs. S. A. Northway.

One pint of milk, a little more than one-half cup of sugar, butter the size of a hickory nut, yolks of three eggs, two teaspoonfuls of corn starch, and flour enough with it to make three-fourths of a cup, one stick of cinnamon, one-half teaspoonful of vanilla; dissolve corn starch and flour in cold milk, add the sugar to the boiling milk, then the other ingredients; pour into a buttered dish and when cold slice and roll in sifted cracker-crumbs, then in egg slightly beaten, then in cracker-crumbs again; drop them into hot lard; they will cook in a moment; sift powdered sugar over them, or they can be served with a sauce.

Charlotte Russe.
Mrs. French, Cleveland.

One pint of good sweet cream, sweetened with one-half cup of sugar, whipped to a stiff froth; dissolve two tablespoonfuls of Cooper's gelatine in warm water; when cool, add this to the beaten cream, and stir until it begins to thicken; set upon the ice to cool. It should be flavored before the cream is beaten.

Charlotte Russe.
Mrs. Powers, Cleveland

One pint of good cream beaten stiff, the whites of two eggs beaten to a stiff froth with one cup of sugar; then put all together, flavoring to taste, and beat thoroughly; stand ladies' fingers up around the sides of a deep dish, pour on the russe and set it on the ice to cool. The cream will thicken quicker if it stands on ice or snow while it is beaten. Or, you may use slices of sponge cake to line your mould, or a loaf of sponge cake may be used, cutting strips from it for the sides and leaving the crust for the top and bottom, each in one piece.

Tapioca Cream.
Miss Flora L ndsley.

Soak two tablespoonfuls of tapioca over night in just enough water to cover; then boil one quart of milk with soaked tapioca in a pail, set in water; add two-thirds of a cup of sugar and a little salt; beat the yolks of three eggs thoroughly; when boiled ten minutes, stir in the yolks, and stir rapidly five minutes to prevent its curdling; flavor, pour in pudding dish, beat the whites of the eggs to a stiff froth, and pour over the top of the cream; sift sugar over the top and brown a few minutes in an oven; serve cold.

Tapioca Cream.
Mrs. J. C. A. Bushnell.

Soak six tablespoonfuls of tapioca in water enough to cover until soft; add one quart of milk and put on top of the stove; beat the yolks of four eggs with four tablespoonfuls of sugar; stir in the tapioca and cook until it thickens, stirring often; beat the whites of the eggs to a stiff froth and add two teaspoonfuls of sugar; spread on top and set in the oven a minute.

Tapioca Cream.
Mrs. B. F. Bowman, Jr.

Put to soak over night three tablespoonfuls of tapioca in a little water or milk; take one pint of milk, let it come to a boil, then stir in the tapioca, and let it boil two or three moments, or until it becomes clear; beat the yolks of two eggs, add a little cold milk to them, then stir in the cream, sweeten and flavor to taste; beat the whites of the eggs to a stiff froth, add a little sugar; put it on the cream and brown.

Rice Custard.
Mrs. B. W. Baldwin.

Boil one-half teacupful of rice in one quart of milk until soft; beat one cup of sugar and three eggs together thoroughly, and add to the rice and milk; boil until it begins to thicken but not curdle; remove from the fire; flavor and pour into glass dish to cool; eaten when very cold, with sponge cake, for lunch or tea.

Apple Cream.
Mrs. S. A. Northway.

Boil twelve apples in water till soft, take off the peel and press the pulp through a hair sieve upon one-half pound of powdered sugar; whip the whites of two eggs, add to the apples, beat all together till it becomes stiff and looks quite white. Serve it heaped up on a dish with a rich custard or cream poured around it.

A Delicate Desert.
Mrs. S. A. Northway.

Lay one-half dozen crackers in a tureen, pour enough boiling water to cover them. In a few minutes they will be swollen three or four times their original size; sprinkle fine sugar and a little nutmeg over them and cover with sweet cream. Serve as sauce for tea.

Imitation Cream.
Mrs. S. A. Northway.

Beat two eggs, one ounce of pulverized sugar, a small piece of butter, with a pint of warm milk; then set it in a water-bath and stir until it acquires the consistency of cream.

Friar's Omelet.

Stew six or seven good-sized apples as for apple sauce; stir in when cooked and still warm, butter the size of a pigeon's egg, and one cupful of sugar; when cold, stir in three well-beaten eggs and a little lemon juice. Now put a small piece of butter into a pan, and when hot, throw in a cupful of bread-crumbs; stir them over the fire until they assume a light brown color. Butter a mould and sprinkle crumbs on the bottom and sides, fill in with apple preparation; sprinkle top with bread-crumbs; bake it for fifteen or twenty minutes, and turn it out on a good-sized platter. It can be eaten with or without sweet sauce.

Ice Cream.
Mrs. D. A. Prentice.

No. 1. To make four quarts of ice cream, take two quarts of new milk, and with the yolks of five eggs and three tablespoonfuls of arrow-root and four cups of sugar, make a custard over a water-bath; when cold, whip into it the whites of the eggs well beaten; then add two quarts of rich cream, which must be well beaten into the custard. Strain and flavor to taste. This is very nice without arrow-root, and more milk can be used in place of the cream.

No 2. Take one quart of cream, one and one-half cups of white sugar; flavor to taste; freeze and serve as usual. This is preferred by some to the cooked custard.

Lemon Ice.
Mrs. McCall.

To one pint of lemon juice add one of water, in which the thin rind of three lemons has been steeped until highly flavored; when partly frozen, add the whites of four eggs, whisked to a stiff froth.

Strawberry Frapees.
Mrs. McCall.

Line a mould with vanilla ice cream, then fill with fresh strawberries; cover with ice cream; cover the mould securely, and pack it in the freezer with pounded ice and salt; let it remain from one-half to three-fourths of an hour, then serve. The fruit must not be frozen, but thoroughly chilled. Ripe peaches peeled and cut are delicious used in this way.

PICKLES.

Pickle Brine.
Mrs. Asa Bailey.

One gallon of water, one quart of salt, one pint of vinegar, two tablespoonfuls of pulverized alum; wash pickles and put in brine as you gather them; when for use, pour boiling water over them; leave until cold, then wipe and put in vinegar.

To Put Down Cucumbers for the Winter.
Mrs. S. A. Northway.

One gallon of vinegar, two gallons of water, two quarts of salt; scald and skim; when cold, put in cucumbers; when the cucumbers are gathered from the vines pour boiling water on them and let them stand until cold. To freshen them, pour boiling hot water over them, and let them stand a day, then treat them as you would cucumbers that have been put down with salt.

Green Color in Pickles.
Mrs. S. A. Northway.

To impart a green color to pickles cover when taken from the vines with boiling hot salt and water, after a short time the water poured off and the pickles drained. They are then to be placed in an earthen pot and covered with boiling vinegar, the top put on and the whole kept at a warm temperature for a long time, the vinegar being poured off every day and heated to boiling and turned upon the pickles again. This is repeated until they are a beautiful green. This vinegar is then poured off, replaced by fresh and the jar tightly closed.

Cucumber Pickles.
Mrs. E. F. Abell.

Make a strong brine and cover them with it three or four days, turning them up from the bottom every morning. Then scald vinegar enough to cover them; whole pepper, cinnamon and mustard seed, a tablespoonful of each, to one and a half gallons of vinegar; take the cucumbers from the brine, drain or dry them on a cloth; pack them in a jar that is to be used, and pour the vinegar scalding hot over them; let them remain two days, pour off the vinegar, scald again, adding a piece of alum the size of a hickory nut to make them crisp. The best cider vinegar should be used. After two days break one open, and if not green through, scald them again. If well covered they will keep for years.

Cucumber Pickles.
Mrs. Henry Prentice.

Make a brine strong enough to bear an egg and put in the cucumbers; let them stand twenty-four hours, then pour off; heat the brine to a boiling point, skim and pour boiling hot over cucumbers; do the same for three mornings, then drain off the brine, pour boiling water over them and then let stand twenty-four hours, then dry off and pack in jars, putting first horse-radish, then pickles, then one gallon of vinegar, one ounce of English mustard, one ounce of whole cinnamon, alum the size of a hickory nut; pour over the pickles hot.

Pickles.
Mrs. A. M. Williams.

For 200 fresh cucumbers, take two gallons of vinegar, six ounces of horse-radish cut in small pieces, one ounce of cloves, one ounce of allspice, two ounces of white mustard seed, two ounces of alum, one pint of salt; boil all the ingredients in the vinegar and pour on the cucumbers.

To Pickle Ripe Cucumbers.
Mrs. S. A. Northway.

Take off the rind and take out the seeds; cut them in slices; place them in weak brine twelve hours, pulverize a piece of alum the size of a hickory nut and put in a kettle of clear water; scald the slices in this solution until you can pierce them with a straw; then to ten pounds of the cucumbers put three pounds of sugar and one quart of vinegar scalded together with the spices, then pour it over the cucumbers.

To Pickle Yellow Cucumbers.

After having peeled the cucumbers and taken out the seeds, cut them into strips and put them in a weak brine of salt and water, with a little alum, for twelve hours; then rinse them off in clear cold water, and to one gallon of vinegar put three pounds of sugar, with mace and cinnamon to your taste. When boiling hot, pour it over the cucumbers. The next day scald it again and pour over. They will be ready for use in a day or two.

French Pickles.
Mrs. M. Baldwin.

One peck of tomatoes, six large onions, put on them after sliced one cup of salt over night; drain them in the morning, boil in two quarts of water and one quart of vinegar fifteen minutes; then drain through a sieve, then add four quarts of vinegar, two pounds of brown sugar, one-half pound of white mustard seed, two tablespoonfuls of ground allspice, two of cloves, two of cinnamon, two of cayenne pepper; mix all, boil fifteen minutes.

Spanish Pickles.
Miss Ada Simonds.

Ten large green peppers, three dozen green cucumbers, one-half peck of green tomatoes; cut in slices, sprinkle with salt, and let stand over night; next day pour off the brine, and add one-half ounce of ground mace, one-half ounce of mustard seed (whole), one-half ounce of ground cloves, three-fourth ounce of celery seed, one pound of grated horseradish, five tablespoonfuls of ground mustard, one pound of brown sugar; cover with cider vinegar and let simmer forty minutes.

Mixed Pickles.
Miss E. Latham.

One peck of sliced green tomatoes, one-fourth peck of small onions, four heads of cauliflower, add small cucumbers and nasturtion seeds; put in layers in salt twenty-four hours, add one pound of white mustard, one pound of French mustard, two teaspoonfuls of white pepper, one-half ounce of cassia buds, one-half ounce of cloves; cover with vinegar; boil twenty minutes, stir while boiling.

Pickled Tomatoes.
Mrs. Allen Houghton.

Slice green tomatoes and boil in weak brine until they are tender; dissolve one pound of brown sugar in one quart of vinegar, scald and pour on the tomatoes; spice to suit the taste.

Tomato Pickles.
Mrs. W. P. Howland.

Two gallons of tomatoes, twelve onions, two pints of vinegar, one pint sugar, two tablespoonfuls of salt, two spoonfuls of ground mustard, two of black pepper, one of allspice, one of cloves.

Chopped Pickle.
Miss H. S. Kellogg.

One peck of green tomatoes, one green pepper, two onions, two heads of cabbage, nine good-sized cucumbers; chop each separately; put in a jar in layers with salt and let stand over night, then wring dry in a piece of cheese cloth; boil five quarts of vinegar with one pound of brown sugar, one-half cup of white mustard seed, one-half cup of black mustard seed, two tablespoonfuls of celery seed, one of ground cloves, one of allspice, one of cinnamon, one teaspoonful of mace or nutmeg; when the vinegar comes to a boil, stir in a cup of English ground mustard, one-half ounce of turmeric mixed with cold vinegar. Pour over the boiling vinegar instead of scalding together.

Chopped Pickle.

One peck of tomatoes, one large head of cabbage, four large onions, two tablespoonfuls of white mustard, two tablespoonfuls of celery seed, one-half of cinnamon, one-half of black pepper; take off both outside slices of tomatoes; slice the rest and chop fine; mix with them three tablespoonfuls of salt, and put in a press for twelve hours, or all night; chop both cabbage and onions fine; mix well together the tomatoes, onions, cabbage and spices; cover with good cider vinegar; keep in a cool place. This will keep a year without being air-tight.

Chow-Chow—Extra.
Mrs. N. E. French.

Two quarts of vinegar, two-thirds of a cupful of ground yellow mustard, one-half cupful of white mustard seed, one coffee cupful of brown sugar, one tablespoonful of celery seed, one teaspoonful of black pepper, one green pepper, one teaspoonful each of cinnamon, cloves, allspice; mix all together and let it come to a boil; then put in the vegetables which have soaked in salt and water two or three hours, one head of cauliflower, two quarts of green tomatoes, cut up one quart of small onions, one quart of celery, one quart of cucumbers. Let it come to a boil.

Chow-Chow.
Mrs. Wm. Gibson.

One-half bushel of green tomatoes, one head of nice cabbage, one dozen or fifteen peppers, one-half peck of onions, one gallon of vinegar, one pound of sugar, all kind of spices. Let it stand ten days, then pour off the liquor, and heat and skim, then pour back.

Pickalillie.
Mrs. S. A. Northway.

Chop fine green tomatoes, add to one gallon after chopped, one teacupful of salt, and let it stand over night; then drain, and add three tablespoonfuls of ground mustard, three of pepper, two of cloves, two of cinnamon, four green peppers, with two or three onions and a little cabbage. Cover with cold vinegar.

Pickalillie.

One peck of green tomatoes, six onions, six green peppers, one cupful of grated horse-radish, one tablespoonful each of allspice, cinnamon and mustard, vinegar enough to cover.

Tomato Relish.
Mrs. Asaph Corter.

Chop one peck of green tomatoes, sprinkle one cupful of salt over them, and let stand over night. In the morning turn off the liquor, place the same in a kettle and cover with vinegar. Chop six green peppers, four onions, one cupful of sugar, one tablespoonful of cloves, one of allspice, one of cinnamon; cook all together until soft.

Tomato Chowder.
Mrs. B. F. Wade.

Twelve ripe tomatoes, four peppers, three onions, two tablespoonfuls of salt, two of sugar, one teacupful of vinegar, cinnamon and cloves to taste; chop all together and boil two hours. The peppers should be most of them ripe.

Pickled Onions.

Select small silver skinned onions. After taking off outside skins, remove with knife one more skin, then put them into strong brine for three days; bring vinegar to a boil, with one or two blades of mace and some whole red peppers. When onions are well drained pour the hot vinegar over them.

Pickled Onions.

Select fine, white onions; let them stand in strong brine four days, changing twice; heat more brine to a boil, throw in onions and boil three minutes; then put them in cold water, and leave four hours; pack in jars with mace, white pepper corns and cloves; then fill with scalding vinegar, to which has been added one cupful of sugar to each gallon; cork while hot.

Pickled Cauliflower.
Mrs. B. F. Bowman, Jr.

Strip off the leaves of the cauliflower, quarter the stalks, and scald them in salt and water until soft, dry them on a sieve and cut in small pieces and place them in a jar, and cover with boiling hot vinegar, add a few cloves, allspice and mustard seed. Cork tight.

Sweet Melon Rind Pickles.

Pare and cut the rind in good shape, soak over night in water with a little salt, cook until soft with a small piece of alum. Drain them well, pour over the sweetened boiling vinegar. Spiced with cinnamon and cloves.

Pickled Peaches.
Mrs. S. A. Northway.

To seven pounds fruit three and one-half pounds sugar (brown is best), one pint vinegar, one ounce cinnamon in stick, once ounce mace in sprig, one ounce whole cloves; rub the peaches, place in a jar; boil the sugar, vinegar and spices together and pour over the fruit; let it stand two days, then pour the vinegar off again, put it on to boil, and when hot put in the fruit and boil until thoroughly heated, or cooked.

Hot Slaw.

One-half cup of sweet cream, one-half cup of vinegar, one head of cabbage, cut fine; yolk of one egg, two even tablespoonfuls of sugar, very little flour, butter size of an egg. Salt the cabbage, and pour hot water over it; after it has stood a few moments, drain and strain the dressing over scalding hot.

Dressing for Cold Slaw.

To the well-beaten yolk of one egg, add a little milk or cream, one-half teacup of vinegar, a small piece of butter. Stir it over the fire until it comes to a boil.

Tomato Catsup.
Mrs. H. L. Hervey.

To one gallon of tomatoes, after the seeds and skins are removed, take one pint of vinegar, one pint of sugar, two tablespoonfuls of cinnamon, one of black pepper, one of cloves, one-half teaspoonful of cayenne pepper, one teaspoonful of salt, one large onion chopped very fine. When your tomatoes are cooked down as thick as you wish, add the vinegar and cook until as thick as before; next add the onions and spices, cook a few moments, take from the stove, and can at once.

Mushroom Catsup.
Mrs. B. F. Bowman, Jr.

Pare and remove the stems of one peck of fresh mushrooms, place in a jar with two tablespoonfuls of salt; let stand over night. In the morning strain through a cloth bag, add enough spice to suit the taste, a little cayenne pepper may be added, which improves it. Do not use any vinegar. Let it boil about fifteen minutes, then bottle and seal.

Chili Sauce.
Mrs. E. A. Sheldon.

Twenty-four large ripe tomatoes, four red peppers, four onions, three tablespoonfuls of salt, six tablespoonfuls of sugar, five cups of vinegar, three tablespoonfuls of cinnamon. Chop tomatoes, onions and peppers fine, put the whole amount together, and boil one hour.

Chili Sauce.
Mrs. A. M. Williams.

Thirty large ripe tomatoes, twelve large ripe onions, twelve green sweet peppers, ten tablespoonfuls salt, twenty tablespoonfuls of sugar, ten teacupfuls of vinegar. Chop fine and simmer to seven quarts. Bottle and seal.

Spiced Fruit.
Mrs. B. F. Bowman, Jr.

To one peck of fruit add seven pounds of sugar (granulated is the best), one and one-half pints of vinegar (dilute if very strong), two tablespoonfuls of ground allspice, two of cloves. Boil vinegar, sugar and spice first, then put in fruit and boil slowly two hours and a half, stirring constantly.

Spiced Grapes.
Mrs. E. F. Mason.

Ten pounds of grapes, four pounds of sugar, one teacup of vinegar, four ounces of cinnamon, two ounces of cloves; scald the liquor and pour over the grapes three successive days.

Spiced Grapes.
Mrs. W. P. Howland.

To ten pounds grapes add six pounds sugar, one pint vinegar, two tablespoons allspice, two of cinnamon, one of pepper, one of cloves, one of salt. Squeeze pulp from grapes and boil twenty minutes, then strain through colander to remove the seeds; stew the skins in a little water and strain through a colander, then spice and boil one-half an hour. Weigh grapes after seeds and skins are removed.

Spiced Citron.
Mrs. D. C. Lewis, Mt. Vernon.

Cut into nice sized pieces and steam until you can pierce with a broom splint; drain in a colander four pounds of white sugar to one quart of vinegar. Scald and skim, then add cinnamon to the taste; let it boil a second time, then put in cans.

Spiced Plums.
Mrs. B. F. Wade.

For a peck of plums, ten pounds of sugar, one-half pint of vinegar, two tablespoonfuls of ground mace, one of cloves, two of cinnamon. Cook until it forms a jelly.

FRUIT JELLIES, PRESERVES, &c.

How to make Fruit Jelly.

The process of all jelly-making is materially the same. Cook the fruit in a porcelain or granite kettle, and stir with a wooden or silver spoon. Iron and tin utensils injure both taste and color. If a brass kettle is used, be particular to scour it thoroughly with hot salt and vinegar just before using, and remove the contents directly on taking from the fire. When the fruit is well softened, with or without the addition of water, according to its nature, turn it into a large, three-cornered bag, that has been wrung out of hot water. The bag may be made of either coarse linen, cotton, or flannel, and must be stout as well as coarse. Suspend this bag of hot fruit over an earthen bowl or jar, and if convenient, in a warm place; leave it to drip for twelve hours. This does away with all the nuisance of squeezing, and the bag being suspended over night, the jelly will only take a little while in the morning to complete. When strained, measure the juice; weigh a pound of sugar to each pint, and be particular about it, too. Don't "guess," if you want to make good jelly, but, if you prefer to measure instead of weigh, use a heaping-pint of sugar for every pint of juice, and, if the fruit is very sour, make the latter measure very scant. Boil the juice fast for twenty minutes, skim it well, then add the sugar, and, when it is dissolved, the jelly will fall from the spoon in flakes; if it does not, then let it boil for five minutes, but it will seldom be necessary. Boiling the juice long after the sugar is put in will make it dark and strong and spoil the jelly. Strain the jelly, while boiling hot, through a thin bag, into a pitcher; hold the bottom of the bag with a fork and twist the top, but not too tight and close, if you want your jelly to be bright and clear. Pour as soon as possible into the molds, as the jelly will form almost immediately, and the quicker it can be transferred the clearer it will be. Dip each mold into cold water before filling, that the form may turn out nicely; and if glass is used, set it on a cloth dipped in cold water, and put in a silver spoon while filling. Keep the cloth cold by frequent dipping and you will never crack a single glass, even if the juice should be boiling hot. Currants and wild cherries in equal quatities make a good and wholesome jelly; red and white currants one of exquisite color, and black currants alone one that is rich and dark and exceedingly palatable. Raspberries to jelly well should be mixed with a third their quantity of currants; cherries and strawberries will not produce a firm jelly without the addition of gelatine, and ripe grapes cannot be depended on. Grapes should be used before they are fully ripened. Gooseberries are also better for jelly while partially green. The late wild plums make a jelly that can scarcely be surpassed either in appearance or flavor. By bruising slightly the juice can be liberated from all these fruits without the use of water, except that which clings to them after rinsing. Crab apples, both the wild and Siberian, and quinces are particularly easy to jelly. Wash and cut them into pieces without peeling or coring; cook in water enough to cover, adding more if necessary to render them perfectly soft. A beautiful amber jelly may be made from tart apples, but it should be flavored with lemon juice. Peaches are not to be relied on. It will require the juice of a lemon to every pint of peach juice, and the jelly may or may not be firm, according to the quality and condition of the peaches.

Lemon Jelly.
Mrs. B. F. Wade.

One quarter pound of sugar, five lemons cut in slices, one quart of boiling water, two oz. gelatine dissolved in one pt. of luke-warm water. Mix all together and strain through a flannel bag and pour in moulds.

Lemon Jelly.

Three pounds sugar, three-quarter pounds butter, one and one-half dozen eggs, one-half dozen the whites left out, one dozen lemons. Grate the rinds of the lemons and press the juice on the sugar, add the butter, and bring it to a boiling heat, then add the eggs, stirring briskly, and the moment it begins to thicken pour it in a cool dish. It will keep for weeks. Use for cake or tarts.

Apple Jelly.
Mrs. Mary King.

Peel and quarter the apples, put them in a preserving kettle, and for every quart of prepared apples allow a pint of water. Cook gently until they are ready to fall apart, then strain through a jelly-bag or cloth, and add to the liquor its weight in sugar. Boil as for other jellies.

To Cook Cranberries.

Put the cranberries to cook with water enough to cover them; let them boil slowly for one hour, then strain through a sieve, put back in the stewpan, and to every cup of juice put one cup sugar. Let it boil for one hour; before taking it up add one and one-half teaspoonfuls of corn starch to every quart of the sauce.

Grape Jelly.

Pick the grapes before they are too ripe, as they become watery then, but they must be ripe enough to have a good flavor, or the jelly will be very acid; pick each grape from the stem, and do not use green or wilted ones: put them over the fire in a porcelain lined kettle, not a brass one, and let them boil up, mashing them well; then strain the juice and measure it, putting it back on the fire, and let it boil thirty or forty minutes; to each pint of juice allow a pound of crushed sugar, which put in the upper oven of the range to warm; when the juice has boiled the time mentioned add the heated sugar, and stir until all is dissolved; then boil ten minutes and test it; if it drops from the spoon thick, it is done. It is very uncertain as to time, therefore difficult to give an exact rule, but should not be boiled more than twenty-five minutes, or it loses its color and flavor.-- *W.*

Apple Compote.

Pare, core, and weigh apples. To one pound of apples allow one pound of sugar and two lemons; parboil apples and cool; pare off nicely with fine knife the yellow rind of lemons, taking care not to break it; put lemon rind in a little saucepan by itself to boil till tender, then set it away to cool: to half-pint water one pound of sugar; when melted set on fire and put in apples, boiling slowly till clear and tender all through, but not till they break; skim the syrup carefully; after taking out apples add lemon peel and juice and boil until transparent; when cold put apples in a glass dish and arrange the peel nicely around them.— *Boston Cook.*

Old-Fashioned Apple Jelly.

Take twenty large juicy apples, pare and chop; put into a jar with the rind (yellow part) of four large lemons, pared thin and cut in bits; cover the jar closely and set in a pot of boiling water; keep water boiling hard all around it until the apples are dissolved; strain through a jelly-bag and mix with the liquid the juice of the four lemons; to one pint of mixed juice one pound sugar; put in kettle, and when sugar is melted set it on the fire, and boil and skim about twenty minutes, or until it is a thick, fine jelly. —*Boston Cook.*

Old-Fashioned Baked Apples.

Take juicy apples, pare and core whole; use a large corer. Put side by side in a baking-pan and fill up centres with brown sugar; pour into each a little lemon-juice, and stick in each a long piece of lemon evenly cut; put enough water in the bottom of the pan to prevent the apples from burning, and bake gently until done.—*Boston Cook.*

Grape Jam.

When the grapes are thoroughly ripe, stem them, then weigh and allow half a pound of sugar to each pound of fruit. Push the pulp from the skins and stew it in a porcelain kettle until it can be easily separated from the seed by straining through a sieve. Put the strained pulp with the skins and juice and a little water into the kettle and cook, closely covered, until the skins are tender. If you were going to can them you would add a teacup or more of water for every pound of fruit, and allow only a pound of sugar to the same quantity. To cook the skins in the syrup toughens them. The sugar must be put in last, but to facilitate matters in canning, the skins can be cooked in the water at the same time the pulp is stewing. In either case add the sugar when the skins are well softened, stir until dissolved, let all boil up well, and seal up immediately in air-tight jars.

To Preserve Wild Plums.

Take wild plums when they are quite ripe and pour boiling water over them to loosen the skins. Let them stand one hour, then slip the skins off, and extract the stones, if you like, or you may leave them in. Allow three-quarters of a pound of sugar to a pound of fruit, and two-thirds of a teacupful of water. Put the fruit and the water over the fire, and let them cook slowly twenty minutes, when add the sugar gradually, and let them boil ten minutes longer. A less quantity of sugar will do, but you will find them better, and they will keep longer, by putting the full allowance of sugar. If you take the stones out of the plums, crack some of them and take the kernels, after blanching them by pouring boiling water over them, and add them to the syrup.

Citron Preserve.

Take out seeds, pare and cut up, and put in water for one night; in the morning put in kettle and simmer, not boil, slowly: the slices should be thin; to one pound of citron one pound of white sugar, quarter of a pound of ginger root, six pounds of fruit; put the ginger, bruised, in a muslin bag; half a lemon to each pound; when the fruit is boiled tender, pour off that water and add sugar, lemon slices and ginger; let it boil slowly till it comes to a jelly; then pour over citron, which should be transparent. The large green melon is better than small ones.—*Boston Cook.*

Green Sweetmeats.
Mrs. Custis, Virginia.

Take watermelon rinds and scald in alum water four hours; cover closely with grape or cabbage leaves; should they be clear and tender then, take them out and throw into cold water; if not, let them boil longer; change this water morning and night until all taste of the alum is extracted; then make a thin syrup of two pounds of sugar to one of fruit; boil it a little and pour it hot over the rinds, and let them stand three days; then boil the sweetmeats until they are transparent and the syrup is quite thick; in the meantime have some white ginger soaked until it is soft enough to be scraped and sliced thin; boil it first in cold water, then in the syrup, together with lemon peel and mace to your taste; tie the ginger in a muslin bag to prevent its coloring the syrup; it is well to put in the grape leaves in layers during the process of scalding, then a layer of rimes; keep kettle closely covered; do not use the juice of the lemons.—*Boston Cook.*

Quince Preserve.

After paring and extracting the cores, quarter and lay in scalding water closely covered for one hour or till tender; this will prevent them from hardening; put parings, seeds, and cores into a preserving kettle, cover with water in which you coddled the quinces and boil one hour, keeping closely covered; to every pint of this liquor, one pound sugar, which, having dissolved in it, put on fire; boil it up and skim; when scum has ceased rising, put in quinces and boil till they are red, tender, and clear all through, but not till they break; keep kettle closely covered if you wish your quinces to be bright colored; if you wish them to be red, put tiny bits of cochineal in a muslin bag; when done take out and spread on a large dish to cool, then put in jars; give syrup another boil-up and it will be like fine jelly; pour it hot over fruit.—*Boston Cook.*

Quince Marmalade.

Six pounds ripe yellow quinces; pare, core, and cut in bits; to one pound cut quince one-half pound sugar; put parings and cores in kettle with water enough to cover; boil slowly to pieces, and strain through a cloth; put in this water quinces; put in bit of cochineal, and boil all over quick fire till a quick, smooth paste, keeping covered, except when skimming—always after skimming; stir up from the bottom; you can, when cold, put this in glass jars, or in deep plates covered with brandied paper; set in lukewarm water when you wish to use it, and the marmalade will turn out easily.—*Boston Cook.*

Preserved Peaches.

Weigh the fruit after it is pared and the stones extracted, and allow a pound of sugar to every one of peaches; crack one quart of the stones, extract the kernels, break them to pieces, and boil in just enough water to cover them until soft, when set aside to steep in a covered vessel; put a layer at the bottom of the kettle, then one of fruit, and so on till you have used up all of both; set it where it will warm slowly until the sugar is melted and the fruit hot through; then strain the kernel water and add it; boil steadily until the peaches are tender and clear; take them out with a perforated skimmer and lay upon large flat dishes, crowding as little as possible. Boil the syrup almost to a jelly—that is, until clear and thick—skimming off all the scum; fill your jars two-thirds full of the peaches, pour on the boiling syrup, and when cold cover with brandy tissue paper, then with cloth, lastly with thick paper tied tightly over them. The peaches should be ready to take off after half an hour's boiling; the syrup boiled fifteen minutes longer, fast, and often stirred to throw up the scum.—*Common-Sense in the Household.*

Quince Soufflé.

Pare, slice, and stew the fruit soft. Sweeten well, and rub through a colander; put into a glass dish; make a custard of one pint of milk, three yolks, and half a cup of sugar. When cold, pour, two inches deep, upon the quince. Whip the whites of the eggs light with sugar and lemon juice, and heap upon the custard.

Spiced Apples.

Eight pounds apples pared, four pounds sugar, one quart vinegar, one ounce stick cinnamon, one-half ounce cloves. Boil the sugar, vinegar, and spices together; put in the apples when boiling and let them remain until tender; take them out and put into a jar; boil down the syrup until thick and pour it over.

Gooseberry Jam.

Stalk and crop six pounds of the small, red, rough gooseberry. Put them into a preserving-pan, and, as they warm, stir and bruise them to bring out the juice. Let them boil for ten minutes; then add four pounds of sugar, and place it on the fire again; let it boil, and continue boiling for two hours longer, stirring all the time to prevent its burning. When it thickens, and will jelly on a plate, it is done enough. Put it into pots and allow it to remain a day before it is covered.

CONFECTIONERY.

Chocolate Caramels. No. 1.
Miss A. M. Lewis.

One cup molasses, two cups brown sugar, boil a few minutes, then add one cup of milk and one-half cup of chocolate beaten together, one tablespoonful of vanilla and a small piece of butter. After putting in the milk and chocolate it must be stirred fast to prevent burning.

No 2.

Two cups molasses, one cup white sugar, one-half cup milk, nearly one-half cup butter, three oz. chocolate, one and one-half teaspoons vanilla.

Molasses Taffy.
Mrs. W. P. Howland.

Four pounds sugar, one pint water, one teaspoon cream tartar, Orleans molasses sufficient to color. Do not stir it.

Cream Candy.
Mrs. W. P. Howland.

Four pounds sugar, one pint water, one teaspoon cream tartar.

Caramels.

One cup white sugar, one of brown sugar, one and one-half molasses, one-half cup grated chocolate, one cup milk, butter size of an egg, melt all together over slow fire, run out into a shallow pan, and divide with a buttered knife.

Marbled Cream Candy.

Four cups white sugar, one cup rich sweet cream, one cup water, one tablespoonful butter, one tablespoonful vinegar, bit of soda the size of a pea, stirred in cream, vanilla extract, three tablespoonfuls of chocolate, grated. Boil all the ingredients except half the cream, the chocolate and vanilla, together very fast until it is a thick, ropy syrup. Heat in a separate sacepan the reserved cream, into which you must have rubbed the grated chocolate. Let it stew until quite thick, and when the candy is done, add a cupful of it to this, stirring it well. Turn the uncolored syrup out upon broad dishes, and pour upon it, here and there, great spoonfuls of the chocolate mixture. Pull as soon as you can handle it with comfort, and with the tips of your fingers only. If deftly manipulated, it will be streaked with white and brown.

Nut Candy.

Cook over a slow fire one pound loaf sugar, one cup water, clear with a little cold vinegar, skim, and when it threads or snaps like glass when raised with a spoon, add any kind of nuts, chopped coacoanut, almonds, hickory nuts or Brazil nuts cut in slices, then pour into a pan and when nearly cold mark in narrow strips with a knife.

Cocoanut Candy quickly made.
Mrs. B. F. Bowman, Jr.

Grate the meat of a coacoanut, and having ready two pounds of finely sifted white sugar, the beaten whites of two eggs, and the milk of the nut; simply mix all together and make into little cakes. In a short while the candy will be dry enough to use.

Taffy.

One cup molasses, one-half cup sugar, one teaspoon vinegar, butter one-half size of nutmeg. Boil ten minutes.

DRINKS.

Coffee.

For seven persons grind one coffee-cupful of freshly browned coffee; mix with it the white of one egg: add one pint of cold water and set the coffee-pot upon the stove where it will heat slowly. Do not let it more than come to the boiling point, or it will be bitter. Add one quart of boiling water just before removing to the table.

Coffee.

To make good coffee have your coffee freshly browned a nice chestnut color, and ground not too fine. Put in a dish as much coffee as would be a heaping tablespoonful for each person, and pour into it enough cold water to moisten the whole, then break into it one or more eggs according to the quantity, one egg is sufficient for ten persons, mix thoroughly and put into your coffee boiler with cold water enough to make the desired quantity. Place the boiler upon the stove, and remove as soon as it comes to a boil. In making large quantities dilute with hot water.

Substitute for Cream in Coffee.
Mrs. H. L. Hervey.

Beat an egg to a froth, add to it a piece of butter the size of a walnut, and turn the coffee on it gradually from the boiling pot into the one for the table, in which it should be previously put. It is difficult to distinguish the taste from fresh cream.

Chocolate.

Six tablespoons grated chocolate to each pint of water; same quantity of milk, sweeten to taste. Rub chocolate smooth in a little cold water and stir into boiling water. Boil twenty minutes, add milk and boil ten minutes more, stirring frequently.

Prepared Cocoa.

Two oz. prepared cocoa, one quart boiling water, one qt. milk; make as you do chocolate, only boil nearly an hour before adding milk, then heating *almost* to boiling. Sweeten to taste.

FOR THE SICK ROOM.

Beef Tea.

One pound lean beef cut into small pieces; put into a jar without a drop of water, cover tightly and set in kettle of boiling water. Heat gradually to a boil and boil for three or four hours, until the meat is like white rags and juice all out. Season with salt, and when cold skim.

Mutton Broth.

Boil one pound lean mutton or lamb unsalted, cut fine in one quart water until it falls to pieces; strain and add one tablespoon soaked rice, simmer one-half hour, then add salt, pepper, four tablespoons milk, then simmer five minutes.

Indian Meal Gruel.

Wet one cup Indian meal and one tablespoon flour to a smooth paste, and stir into two quarts of boiling water; boil half an hour, salt to taste, sugar and nutmeg if liked. Oat meal gruel the same way.

Milk Porridge.

Boil a paste made of one tablespoon meal, one of flour, in two cups of boiling water twenty minutes, add two cups milk, and cook ten minutes more.

Graham Hasty Pudding.

One cup Graham flour wet with cold water, stirred into one large cup boiling water, boil ten minutes, stirring constantly; add one large cup milk, and boil ten minutes longer.

A plain dessert for grown people or children with milk, sugar and nutmeg, as one prefers.

Calves-foot Jelly.

Boil four nicely cleaned calves-feet in three quarts of water until reduced to one, very slowly; strain and set away until cold, then take off the fat from the top and remove the jelly into a stew-pan, avoiding the settlings, and adding half a pound of white powdered sugar, the juice of two lemons, and the whites of two eggs—the latter to make it transparent. Boil altogether a few moments and set away in bowls or glasses; it is excellent in a sick room.

Dried Flour for Teething Children.

One cup of flour tied in a stout bag dropped into cold water, then set over a fire. Boil three hours steadily; turn out the flour ball and dry in the hot sun all day; or, if you need it at once, dry in a moderate oven without shutting the door.

TO USE IT:

Grate a tablespoonful for a cupful of boiling milk and water (half and half). Wet up the flour with a very little cold water, stir in and boil five minutes. Put in a little salt.

Mountain Custard.

Sweeten and flavor a pint of milk to taste. When lukewarm, add two teaspoonfuls of rennet wine. If it does not set in an hour, add more wine. It should be smooth and thick like a baked custard.

Beef Tea.
Mrs. H. L. Hervey.

Take one pound of lean beef, pound well or cut in very thin slices, put in a glass fruit-jar and cover with water; put the jar in a kettle of cold water, and after the water in the kettle comes to a boil, let it boil for several hours, not less than three. If it is needed sooner, a little may be poured from the jar into a bright tin basin and cooked for a moment or two. Salt to taste; it is then ready for use. If needed very strong, put more beef in the jar and no water. It is best made in small quantities.

Beef Extract.
Mrs. J. A. Garfield.

One pound lean beef cut fine and put in one pint of cold water and six drops muriatic acid; after being thoroughly mixed it is allowed to stand one hour, and then strained and pressed until all the liquid is extracted.

Mutton Broth.

To one pound of lean mutton (cut off all the fat) use one quart water and a little salt, with a few crusts of bread; boil slowly for a couple of hours, then skim off the oily matter carefully before using.

Corn Meal Gruel.

Take one-half pint meal, pour over it one pint or more, of cold water, stir up, let settle a moment, pour off the water, repeat this until there is nothing left but the yellow grains; then put the washed meal into two pints cold water, and place where it will boil; cook two hours, and when done, add a pinch of salt. It may be eaten with or without other seasoning.

Jellice.

One-half teaspoon of currant, lemon or cranberry jelly put into goblet, beat well with two tablespoons water, fill up with ice water, and you have a refreshing drink for a fever patient.

Oat Meal Gruel.

Put two heaping tablespoons oat meal in one quart cold water; stir till it commences to boil, then cook one hour, stirring occasionally. Do not let it scorch; season with salt, sugar, and spice desired. For infants and very sick patients it must be strained, and not salted.

Tapioca Jelly.

One-half pint tapioca, one quart water, juice and some of the grated rind of a lemon; soak the tapioca for three or four hours in the water, sweeten it and boil for one hour in a custard kettle, or until quite clear, stirring it often. When almost done, stir in the lemon, and when sufficiently cooked, pour into moulds. Serve with sweetened cream.

Drink for the Sick.

Two tablespoons of arrow-root in a quart pitcher with a little cold water, three tablespoons white sugar, the juice of one lemon and part of the rind; stir all quickly while pouring boiling water, until the pitcher is full; drink cold.

Apple Water.

Slices of apple put in warm water with a little sugar make a pleasant drink.

Panada.

Six Boston crackers, split, two tablespoons white sugar, a good pinch of salt, and a little nutmeg, enough boiling water to cover them well. Split the crackers and pile in a bowl in layers, salt and sugar scattered among them; cover with boiling water and set on the hearth, with a close top over the bowl, for at least one hour. The crackers should be almost as clear and soft as the jelly, but not broken. Eat from the bowl, with more sugar sprinkled in if you wish it. If properly made, this panada is very nice.

Cup Pudding.

One tablespoon of flour, one egg; mix with cold milk and a pinch of salt to a batter. Boil fifteen minutes in a buttered cup. Eat with sauce, fruit or plain sugar.

Cracked Wheat.

Boil slowly for one-half hour a small teacup of cracked wheat with a little salt, in one quart of hot water, stirring often. Serve with sugar and cream or new milk.

Arrow-root Custard.

One tablespoon arrow-root, one pint of milk, one egg, two tablespoons sugar; mix the arrow-root with a little of the cold milk, put the rest of the milk on the fire and boil and stir in the arrow-root and egg and sugar, well beaten together; scald and pour into cups to cool. Any flavoring the invalid prefers may be added.

Cream Soup.

One pint boiling water, one-half teacup cream, add broken pieces of toasted bread, a little salt.

Sago Jelly Pudding.

Wash thoroughly one teacup of sago, cook it in three pints of water fifteen or twenty minutes till perfectly clear, add a very little salt; stir in half a glass of currant, grape, or other jelly, and two spoonfuls sugar. Mould and serve cold, with cream and sugar, or eat warm.

Refreshing and Cooling Wash for the Sick Room.

Take of rosemary, wormwood, lavender, rue, sage and mint, a large handful of each, place in a stone jar, and turn over it one gallon of strong cider vinegar, cover closely and keep near the fire for four days; then strain and add one ounce pounded camphor gum. Bottle and keep tightly corked.

Chicken Jelly.

One-half of a raw chicken, pounded with a mallet, bones and meat together, plenty of cold water to cover it well, about a quart. Heat slowly in a covered vessel, and let it simmer until the meat is in white rags and the liquid reduced one-half. Strain and press, first through a colander, then through a coarse cloth. Salt to taste, and pepper if you think best; return to the fire, and simmer five minutes longer; skim when cool. Give to the patient cold—just from the ice—with unleavened wafers. Keep on the ice. You can make into sandwiches by putting the jelly between thin slices of bread spread lightly with butter.

Milk Porridge.

Two cups best oat meal, two cups water, two cups milk. Soak the oat meal over night in the water; strain in the morning, and boil the water half an hour. Put in the milk with a little salt, boil up well and serve. Eat warm, with or without powdered sugar.

Thickened Milk.

With a little milk, mix smooth a tablespoonful of flour and a pinch of salt. Pour upon it a quart of boiling milk, and when it is thoroughly amalgamated put all back into the sauce-pan, and boil up once, being careful not to burn, and stirring all the time, to keep it perfectly smooth, and free from lumps. Serve with slices of dry toast. It is excellent in diarrhea and becomes a specific by scorching the flour before mixing with the milk.

Wine Whey.
Mrs. C. S. Simonds.

Take half a pint of new milk, put it on the fire, and the moment it boils pour in two glasses of wine and a teaspoonful of powdered sugar previously mixed. The curd will soon form, and after it has boiled set aside till the curd settles; pour the whey off and add a pint of boiling water. Sweeten to the taste. Set upon ice to cool. This is a very acceptable drink to patients suffering from fevers or debility.

Ginger Beer.

Two gallons of water, one quart of molasses, one tablespoonful of ginger, one-half tablespoonful of cloves, one-half tablespoonful cream of tartar, one pint of yeast; steep hops and wintergreen.

Blackberry Wine.
Mrs. Mary King.

Mash the berries and pour over one qt. of boiling water to each gallon; let the mixture stand twenty-four hours, stirring occasionally; then strain and measure into a keg or jug, adding two pounds sugar to each gallon. Let it stand in a cold place about a week, then draw off. Cork tight and let it stand until the following October, when it will be ready for use. It is especially useful for Summer complaint.

Milk and Rice Gruel.

Wet two tablespoons ground rice with cold milk, stir it into one quart boiling milk and boil ten minutes; add a little salt.

Cough Syrup.

The following recipe is sent by a valued friend who has found it very efficient in her family in curing coughs. Tincture of blood root, two ounces; tincture of lobelia, two ounces; tincture of tolu, two ounces; essence of anise, three drachms; essence of wintergreen, one drachm; two quarts of molasses. Dose, one teaspoonful every three hours, or oftener as the case may require.

Raspberry Shrub.

Put raspberries in a porcelain kettle, and scarcely cover them with vinegar, adding one pint of sugar to a pint of juice, scald, skim, and bottle when cool.

Dyspepsia

Is cured by muscular exercise, voluntary or involuntary, and in no other way can it be cured, because nothing can create or collect the gastric juice except exercise; it is a product of the human machine. Nature only can make it.

For Croup.

Take a knife or grater, and grate or shave in small particles, about a teaspoonful of alum; mix with it about twice its quantity of sugar, to make it palatable, and administer it as quick as possible. Almost instantaneous relief will be afforded.

Hoarseness.

Bake a lemon or sour orange for twenty minutes in a moderate oven, then open it at one end and dig out the inside, and sweeten it with sugar and molasses and eat. This will cure hoarseness and remove pressure from the lungs.

Sago Custard.

Soak two tablespoons sago in a tumbler of water an hour or more, then boil in the same water until clear, and add a tumbler of sweet milk; when it boils add sugar to taste, then a beaten egg and flavoring.

Baked Milk.

Bake two quarts of milk for eight or ten hours in a moderate oven, in a jar covered with writing paper, tied down. It will then be as thick cream, and may be used by weak persons.

Egg Gruel.

Beat the yolk of an egg with a tablespoon of sugar, beating the white separately; add a teacup of boiling water to the yolk, then stir in the white, and add any seasoning; good for a cold.

To remove Grease from Broths for the Sick.

After pouring in dish, pass clean white paper quickly over the top of broth, using several pieces, until all grease is removed.

Beef Tea and Rice.

During war times I was always making this for the invalided men whose appetites were returning. Take an ounce of Carolina rice, wash it carefully in two waters, and pick out the grit or bleaks; put it in a pie plate with half a pint of cold beef tea, or beef broth, and let it swell over night; next day bake just as it is until well done; forty minutes in a quick oven does it; watch it, however, and add more broth if it gets hard; boil the third of a pint of milk, and when it is cool beat an egg into it; then mix this with your rice; season with a very little salt and but a few grains of pepper; let it be put back in the oven and bake again slowly for an hour. This is highly nutritive and easily digested.—*One who has nursed a great deal.*

Magic Toothache Drops.

Chloroform, one part; oil of cloves, one part; spirits of camphor, two parts; mix, and apply so the decayed tooth on a bit of soft cotton. We know of nothing to equal this mixture for toothache, and we have seen it used a great deal.

Neutralizing Mixture for Dysentery.

Pulverized Rhubarb, one oz.; Soda, one oz.; essence peppermint, one oz.; one-half pint brandy; one pint boiling water. Sweeten.

Fits.

Salt put into the mouth will instantly relieve the convulsive movements in fits, either in children or animals, and the frequent use of salt is the best remedy for *Epilepsy.*

Disinfectant.

One pound sulphate of iron (common copperas) and eight ounces of crude carbolic acid dissolved in one gallon of water. The whole will not cost more than a dime. This compound will keep away every flea from the barnyard, if sprinkled over the surface from a common watering pot, and render the smell inoffensive. Poured in a defective drain or cesspool, they will become odorless. Flies will keep away from its vicinity. This simple remedy, used in every yard, will work more for the sanitary good of the city than all the money that it takes to run this entire force.

Disinfectant.

One pound green copperas, dissolved in one quart of water, will concentrate and destroy the foulest smells; copperas dissolved in the bed-vessels of the sick room, will clean the vessel, neutralize the poisonous gases, and prevent the spread of contagious diseases. Wherever there are offensive, putrid gases, dissolve copperas and sprinkle it about, and in a few days they will pass away. If a cat, rat or mouse dies about the house, place some dissolved copperas in an open vessel near the place where the nuisance is, and it will purify the atmosphere.

Poison Antidotes.

For oxalic acid, chalk, magnesia, or soap and water. For alkali, the best remedy is vinegar. For corrosive sublimate, one-half dozen raw eggs, beside the emetic, the latter to be made of one heaping teaspoonful of common salt, with one of ground mustard in a glass of cold water, swallowed instantly. When it has acted, swallow whites of two raw eggs. If poisoned from laudanum, a cup of strong coffee after emetic. If arsenic, one-half cup sweet oil or melted lard after the emetic.

To Stop Flow of Blood.

Bind the cut with cobwebs and brown sugar pressed on like lint. Or, if these are not procurable, use fine dust of tea. When stopped, apply laudanum.

Ointment for Chapped Hands.

Four ounces glycerine, one-fourth ounce white wax, one dram camphor gum (pulverized), one-half dram carbolic acid. Heat the glycerine boiling hot, add the wax, then thicken to a jelly with corn starch, dissolve the starch in a little water, add the camphor gum, then take from the stove, add the acid and stir until cold.

Cure for Chilblains.

One dram sugar of lead, two drams white vitriol, powder and add four ounces water. Apply every evening.

Ear-ache Remedy.

Take a little honey, put it in a piece of writing paper, boil it over top of lamp chimney, and put in a spoon and turn two or three drops into the ear.

White Balsam Salve.

One pound of resin, three ounces beeswax, four ounces tallow (for green add one-fourth ounce verdigris).

Inflammation Salve.

Four ounces resin, four ounces castile soap, four ounces beeswax, two ounces spirits of camphor, one ounce oil of hemlock. Melt together. It is excellent.

Genuine Hop Bitters.

One-half ounce buchu leaves, one-half ounce dandelion root, one pint whisky, one-half pint hops (or more), five pints water; simmer together and add liquor.

Wash for the Hair.

Twenty drops ammonia, one-half ounce borax, one-half ounce saltpetre, one-half ounce carbonate potassa, soft water one quart.

MISCELLANEOUS.

Beef Brine.
Mrs. E. C. Wade.

For 100 pounds beef, six gallons water, six pounds salt, three pounds brown sugar, one pint molasses, three of saltpetre (pulverized), one of soda. Mix all together and pour on the beef. Salt dissolves most readily in cold water.

If the beef is for drying, less salt is required, four and one-half pounds being sufficient.

To Cure Hams.
Miss R. P. Dean.

For every 100 pounds of meat, take eight pounds salt, one ounce saltpetre, two ounces soda, one quart molasses, and pure rain or spring water enough to cover the meat to the depth of four or five inches. Boil and skim well and put on cold. The hams may remain in this pickle from five to seven weeks, according to size. This is also an excellent pickle for beef to dry.

For Laying Down Eggs.

Mix one-half pint of unslacked lime with one pint of common salt; pour over it two gallons of boiling hot water; put in a stone jar with a cover; when it is cool, put your eggs in, and all that come to the top take out, as they will not keep. Be careful and do not crack them, as that would spoil the brine. Put them in two or three at a time, slowly.

To Preserve Eggs.

Take a patent pailful of spring water, pour it into a stone jar, take one pound of lime, one pint of salt; let it stand for three days, stir it every day, then pour it off and put in your eggs.

To Sour Vinegar Quick.

If any one wants vinegar to sour quick and be sharp, put a good large handful of sugar in your jug, and let it be kept in a warm place; in the Summer, out doors where the sun strikes is a good place. If you put plenty of sugar in, you can once in awhile put a cup of water in also, and you will never know it is there.

Shaving Soap.

A very fine shaving soap solution may be made by taking a quarter pound of white castile soap in shaving, one pint of rectified spirit, one gill of water; perfume to taste. Put in a bottle, cork tightly, set in warm water for a short time, and agitate occasionally till the solution is complete. Let stand, pour the liquid off the dregs, and bottle for use.

Starch Polish.

Put two ounces of gum arabic in a pitcher, pour one pint of boiling water over it and cover; let it stand until the following day, then turn it off from the dregs in the bottles and cork.

Two tablespoonfuls stirred into a pint of starch made in the usual way (either hot or cold), will give a fine gloss to linen.

Indelible Ink.

Six cents worth (a little stick) of nitrate of silver, dissolved in one tablespoon of vinegar; starch stiff the part of garment to be marked in cold starch, putting in a little soda, and iron smooth and dry. It will be yellow when dry. Use the ink with a fine pen. Let it lie one-half hour after marked before putting in water. Will keep bright as long as garment lasts.

Cure for Burns.

Sprinkle the burn with baking powder and cover with a wet cloth. When only superficial, the pain will cease instantly with one application; when deeper, longer time and more applications will be needed; or keep the part covered with common molasses until one-third part linseed oil and two-thirds lime-water can be procured, then apply and wrap in soft linen.

Cologne Water.

One dram oil rosemary, one dram oil lemon, one-half dram oil bergamot, one-half dram oil lavender, twenty-five drops tincture musk, four drops oil cinnamon, four drops oil cloves, one-half pint alcohol.

Washing Fluid.

One pound concentrated potash, one ounce carbonate ammonia, one ounce salts of tartar. Dissolve in two gallons of water.

Cheap Blueing.

One-fourth ounce oxalic acid, one-half ounce Prussian blue, dissolved in one quart soft water.

Bleaching Solution.

Take sal soda, three pounds; chloride of lime, one pound; water, one gallon. Boil the sal soda in the water ten or fifteen minutes, or till it is thoroughly dissolved; then remove from the fire and stir in the chloride of lime. When cool and thoroughly settled, turn off the clear liquor into a jug, cork tightly, and set in cool place. Use for removing fruit stains, etc., from white linen and cotton goods.

For Bleaching Cloth.

Take one-half pound chloride of lime to fifteen yards of cloth. Boil your cloth in soap-suds, then suds and rinse it. Put your lime into a cloth and rub through hot water; pour your lime water into enough cold water that your cloth will not be crowded. Let your cloth stand in it nine hours, stirring occasionally; then rinse thoroughly; boil again in suds, suds, rinse and dry.

To Wash Clothes without Fading.

Wash and peel Irish potatoes and then grate them in cold water. Saturate the articles to be washed in this potato water, and they can then be washed with soap without any running of color. This will set the color in carpets if oil or grease is to be taken out and the colors are apt to run. This will set the colors in figured black muslin, colored merinos, stockings, ribbons, and other silk goods. Often the potato water cleanses sufficiently without the use of soap. In woolen goods it is necessary to strain the water, else the particles will adhere; but this is not necessary in goods from which they can be well shaken.

To Wash Doubtful Calicoes.

Put a teaspoon of sugar of lead in a pail of water and soak fifteen minutes before washing.

To Set the Colors in Calicoes and Stockings.

Put some sugar of lead in the water when you wash them, and a little ammonia in the water to rinse them. It will set the color.

To Clean Hairbrushes.

Put a teaspoonful of ammonia in a pint of warm water, and shake the brushes through it; when they look white, rinse in clear water, and dry in the sun or a warm place.

Hair-brushes that have become soft with long use can be stiffened by cleaning the bristles thoroughly with a little bicarbonate of soda and water, rinsing well, and then soaking the bristles in cold alum water for a few hours, and then drying. It will make an old brush about as good as new.

To Remove Glass Stoppers.

Put on a drop of oil on top of bottle around stopper.

To Cut Glass.

Lay the glass on a piece of twine or whipcord; heat an iron (an old file will do) red-hot; place the iron on the glass over the string for a few seconds, when the glass will break off as smooth as if it was cut with a diamond.

Mucilage.

This is a mucilage which will unite wood or mend porcelain or glass: To eight and one-half ounces of a strong solution of gum arabic add thirty grains of a solution of sulphate of alumina dissolved in three-quarters of an ounce of water.

A Useful Table for Housewives.

Flour—One pound is one quart. Meal—One pound and two ounces is a quart. Butter—One pound is one quart. Powdered white sugar—One pound and one ounce is one quart. Ten eggs are a pound. A common tumbler holds half a pint. A teacup is a gill.

To Remove Old Putty.

When a light of glass has been broken, and the window requires a new pane of glass, it is often very hard to remove the old putty—that is, unless you know how to remove it. Take a hot iron and draw it along on the putty very slowly, and you will find that the putty has become soft, and you can remove it with a knife without any trouble.

To prevent Potatoes from shriveling up in Spring and Summer.

Take the potatoes early in the Spring before they begin to sprout, and put them into a tub or barrel, and pour boiling hot water on them, and let them stand till cold, then spread them out to dry, and put them away in a cool place. The hot water kills the eye, or germ of the potato, and prevents its sprouting and absorbing the substance of the potato. This method has been in use by a few persons for some years, but we believe this is the first time it has been published for the benefit of all.

Airing Pillows.

Do not put your pillows in the sunlight to air, but in a shady place, with a clear, dry wind blowing over them. If it is cloudy, and yet not damp, and the wind not strong, it is all the better. This, if practiced often, keeps well-cured feathers always sweet. A hot sun in the best of feathers will turn them rancid.

To Kill Moths in Feathers.

Bake the feathers in the oven, not too hot.

To Cleanse Bottles.

Dissolve one ounce of chloride of lime in one quart of water, and fill the bottles with the liquid; set them aside for several days, and rinse them well with water. The water of the chloride of lime can be used several times. For bottles which are not very dirty, use one part of muriatic acid diluted with three parts of water. Sawdust put into bottles, and some water added, will clean well, especially such bottles as have contained oil.

To Clean Decanters.

When making cake or omelette, take your discarded eggshells, crush them into small bits, put them into your decanters three parts filled with cold water, and thoroughly shake them. The glass will look like new, and all kinds of glass washed in the same water, will look equally well.

Traveling Lunch.

Sardines chopped fine, also a little ham, a small quantity of chopped pickles, mix with mustard, pepper, catsup, salt, and vinegar; spread between bread nicely buttered. To be like jelly cake, cut in slices crossways.

To Remove Ink Stains.

Sponge stains thoroughly with skim milk, then wash out milk, with a clean sponge and cold water, then in warm water, and rub dry with a cloth. Dry ink stains can be removed with oxalic acid or lemon juice and salt.

To remove ink stains from cloth, dip the stain into hot fat, lard or tallow, and when cold wash out in hot water, and it will usually remove the stain.

To Remove Ink Stains from Printed Books.

Procure a pennyworth of oxalic acid, which dissolve in a small quantity of warm water, then slightly wet the stain with it, when it will disappear, leaving the leaf uninjured.

Mosquitos.

To get rid of these tormentors, take a few hot coals on a shovel, or a chafing dish, and burn upon them some brown sugar in your bedrooms and parlors, and you effectually banish or destroy every mosquito for the night.

To drive away Ants.

Place a saucer of ground cloves where they are troublesome, and they will disappear.

Sprigs of wintergreen or ground ivy will drive away red ants; branches of wormwood will serve the same purpose for black ants.

To Expel Rats.

Make a strong solution of copperas water and paint the walls of the whole cellar. Then pound up copperas and scatter it along the side of the walls and into every hole where it can be thrown.

Cement for Broken China.

A bit of isinglass dissolved in gin or boiled in spirits of wine, will make strong cement for broken glass, china and seashells.

To Kill Worms and Slugs.

Take an ordinary sprinkling pail with a free nozzle, put in a few spoonfuls of kerosene, and two or three spoonfuls of helebore, then fill with water and give the bushes a thorough sprinkling. Take care to have the mixture reach the under side of the leaves. Apply as soon as the slugs appear.

Cement for Broken China.

Make a thick solution of gum arabic in water, then stir in plaster of Paris until the mixture becomes a sticky paste. Apply with a brush to the broken edges, put together, and in three days the article cannot be broken in the same place.

To Mend China.

Take a very thick solution of gum arabic in water, and stir into it plaster of Paris until the mixture becomes of a proper consistency. Apply it with a brush to the fractured edges of the china and stick them together. In three days the articles cannot be broken in the same place. The whiteness of the cement renders it doubly valuable.

Iron dust may be removed by oxalic acid dissolved in water, or by salt mixed with lemon juice and placed in the sun. If necessary apply twice.

Iron rust spots on cloth can be removed by rubbing on lemon juice, and putting the cloth in the sun to dry, and then rinse with clear water, and repeat the process if it is not all out.

To Remove Rust from a Stovepipe.

Rub with linseed oil (a little goes a great way); build a slow fire till it is dry. Oil in the Spring to prevent it from rusting.

To Clean Tinware.

Common soda is excellent for cleaning tinware. Dampen a cloth, dip it in soda and rub briskly, then wipe dry.

Kerosene and powdered lime, whiting, or wood ashes will scour tins with the least labor.

To Clean Brass.

Immerse or wash it several times in sour milk or whey. This will brighten it without scouring. It may then be scoured with a woolen cloth dipped in ashes.

Common whiting, wet with ammonia, rubbed on a piece of flannel, will clean silverware beautifully.

To take White Stains from Dark Wood.

Use equal parts of vinegar, sweet-oil, and spirits of turpentine; shake all well together in a bottle; apply with a flannel cloth and rub dry with old silk or linen.—*G. D. S.*

Wine Stains on Marble.

Let the slab be placed where it will get as warm as it will bear, cover it with gum arabic dissolved into a paste; two or three applications will take out oil.

To Remove Stains, Spots, etc., from Clothing.

It is frequently quite important to remove paint stains, etc., from clothing, and it is not always an easy thing to do. It is quite easy to remove fresh paint from clothing, provided you remove the oil as well as the white lead, or whatever is used as color or body for the paint. By using benzine, turpentine, alcohol, etc., to remove paint, you thin out the oil and spread it over a larger surface, and by brushing and rubbing you generally remove the lead or paint color, but leave a good deal of the oil in the cloth, which does not evaporate with the benzine or turpentine.

To remove paint from cloth, use benzine, alcohol, or rectified spirits of turpentine to thin out the oil, and try to confine it to as small a space on the cloth as possible. Try to get the oil out of the goods as well as the paint; and when you have removed all the paint, try to remove all the oil by pressing the cloth between folds of coarse blotting paper, or by rubbing in dry fuller's earth to absorb the oil, and brushing it out and repeating the process. If you can use soap without injury to the goods it will assist greatly in removing the oil. If the paint has become dry, remember that chloroform is a powerful solvent, and will often remove paint stains when everything else has failed; but also remember that you must remove the oil after it has been dissolved, or you will still have a spot. Always place a cloth or piece of coarse blotting paper underneath the cloth you are cleaning, which will absorb a great deal of the oil.

Butter, lard, and grease of that kind, can be removed from silk and other goods by placing it between two pieces of blotting paper and pressing it with a warm flat-iron; also by rubbing in dry fullers' earth to absorb the grease, and brushing it out and repeating the process. Pulverized French chalk is also good for the same purpose.

Fruit stains are often very easily removed, and at other times they are almost indelible. Lemon juice will often remove the stain. Tartaric acid is also good. Sometimes a weak solution of chloride of lime will be sufficient to remove the stain.

Acid stains can generally be removed by the use of aqua ammonia. Chloroform will often restore the color where it has been destroyed by acids. Aqua ammonia will remove the stain of iodine from the skin or clothing.

To Take Stains out of White Goods.

One teaspoon chloride of lime, dissolved in three quarts of water, will take any kind of stains out of white goods. Put the part with the stain on it in the water; let it remain in until out. It will not injure the goods when prepared in this way.

To Take Mildew from Linen.

Dip the stained cloth in butter-milk and lay in the sun; or, rub the spots with soap, scrape chalk over it and rub it well; lay it on the grass in the sun; as it dries, wet it a little; it will come out with two applications.

To remove stains of acids, use hartshorn and alkalis.

Chloroform will remove grease stains from light silk or poplin without changing the color.

A Ready Grease Exterminator for Woolens.

One ounce pulverized borax, one-half ounce gum camphor, one quart boiling water; shake well and bottle.

To Clean Very Dirty Black Dresses.

Two parts soft water to one of alcohol; soap a sponge well, dip in mixture and rub the goods; iron on wrong side while damp, after sponging off with hot water.

To Renovate Faded and Worn Garments.

To one quart alcohol add one-fourth pound extract logwood, two ounces loaf sugar, one-fourth ounce blue vitriol; heat gently till all are dissolved, then bottle for use.

Directions.—To one pint boiling water put three or four teaspoons of the mixture, and apply to the garment with a clean brush, wetting the fabric thoroughly; let dry, then suds out well and dry again to prevent cracking; brush with the nap to give polish. May be applied to silks and woolens having colors, but most applicable to gentlemen's apparel.

To Dress Silk.

Take an old kid glove as near the color of the dress as possible; put it in a sauce-pan with a quart of water; boil down to a pint and sponge the dress on the right side with this. It is the dressing the French give to many of their silks. A white glove will do for any color if you cannot match the shade.

A bit of glue dissolved in skim-milk will restore old crape.

To Clean Feathers.

To clean feathers from animal oil and the disagreeable odor often noticed in them, make a lime water by mixing one pound of fresh slaked lime with three or four gallons of water, and let stand three or four hours, and pour off the clear liquor for use. Put the feathers into a tub and pour on sufficient clear lime water to cover them; let them stand in the lime water two or three days, and then rinse the feathers in clear water and dry them. When thoroughly dried, the feathers should be whipped or beaten till they are loose and nice. Old feathers are often cleaned in this way.

Curling Plumes.

Put some coals of fire on a shovel, sprinkle brown sugar on the coals, and hold the plumes in the smoke. One application will be sufficient to make them as nice as new.

Take a little salt and sprinkle it upon the hot stove, and hold the plume over the smoke a few minutes. It will be curled.

To Clean Coffee and Spice Mills.

Grind a tablespoonful of rice through the mill and it will be thoroughly cleaned.

Self Holder for a Spoon.

In dropping medicine into a spoon, place the handle between the leaves of a closed book lying on the table, and then both hands may be used in dropping the mixture.

Never enter a room where a person is sick with an infectious disease, with an empty stomach.

Different Uses for Ammonia.

No house-keeper should be without a bottle of spirits of ammonia, for besides its medicinal value, it is very desirable for household purposes. It is nearly as useful as soap, and its cheapness brings it within the reach of all.

Put a teaspoon of ammonia into a quart of warm soap suds, dip in a flannel cloth and wipe off dust and fly specks, and see how much labor you can save.

With a pint of suds mix a teaspoon of the spirits, dip in your silver spoons, forks, etc., rub them with a soft brush, and polish with a chamois skin.

For washing windows and mirrors, put a few drops of ammonia on a piece of paper, and it will readily take off every spot or finger mark on the glass.

It is a most refreshing agent on the toilet table. A few drops in a basin will make a better bath than pure water, and, if the skin is oily, it will remove its glossiness and disagreeable odors, often arising from the feet in hot weather, nothing is better for cleansing the hair of dandruff and dust.

For cleansing hair and nail brushes it is equally good: Put a teaspoon of ammonia into a pint of warm water and shake the brushes through the water, when they look white rinse them in cold water, and put them in the sunshine or a warm place to dry, the dirtiest brushes will come out white and clean.

THE BIRD FANCIER.
A Chapter on the Care and Culture of Canaries.

A tuneful, sweet-voiced Canary Bird is one of the choicest and most delightful pets that a cultured lady can possess. It is a source of much refined pleasure and amusement, and well repays the care necessary to make it a hardy, happy and melodious member of the household.

The following simple instructions in the care of Canaries will be found useful to all lovers of the feathered songsters:

1. *Of Choosing the Birds.*—Don't be particular as to color, brown or mottled birds often prove the best singers. Avoid birds with red eyes; they are delicate and not easily kept in song. Tameness is not a sign of excellence; a bird that is moderately shy and spry will be likely to turn out best. Look for melody and sweetness rather than loud, shrill tones, if the canary is intended for a private house. Be sure that the little fellow's legs and feet are clean and perfect—and when you buy a bird take it home yourself, and not leave it for the dealer to send. Thus you will be sure to get the one you select. For singing, get a male bird. The sex may be determined in a brood containing both male and female, by comparing the birds. The male's plumage is brightest in color; his head is larger and longer; his body more slender; his neck longer; his legs longer and straighter than those of the female, and the feathers about his temples and eyes are brighter than elsewhere upon his body.

2. *Of Taming.*—Carry your bird home carefully and gently. Have its cage ready and furnished with seed and water. Let it step of its own accord out of the temporary cage into its new home. Place a light in front of the cage, and without going too near or seeming to watch the bird, chirp or whistle to encourage it. The chances are that he will begin to sing at once. If it sulks a little at the start, so much the better, but if the shyness continues after the first day, catch the bird and immerse it in the water of its bath-tub, then leave it to itself. In drying and smoothing its feathers it will forget its homesickness and make itself comfortable.

3. *Of Cages.*—The wire bell-shaped cage is best for song birds. Brass is better than painted wire. In addition to the bath-tub and seed cup, the cage should have two or three perches, made of cane or hard wood, made round and smooth. These should be placed across the cage in such positions that one will never be exactly over another

to catch the litter. Keep the perches clean by frequent washings with yellow soap and water, and never return to the cage until thoroughly dry. At least twice a week the bottom of the cage must be taken off and washed, and the bottom covered with fine sand or gravel. Be careful never to use *salt water* sand. Never hang the cage in a draft of air (as in an open window), or in the hot sun without protecting the bird by some sort of shelter on the windy side and at the top. Never hang the cage out of doors in wet weather. In Winter never leave the cage in a room without a fire. *Don't leave the care of your bird and cage to servants.*

4. *Of Baths.*—Let the water be fresh daily. Canaries will not bathe in stale or dirty water. The bath-tub should be of such size that it will pass easily through the cage door—and it should be removed as soon as the bird has bathed. If you have a wire cage with a bottom that hooks on, a good plan is to fill the bath-tub and set it on the floor or an old table. Then unhook the bottom of the cage, and place the cage with the bird in it over the bath-tub. The bird will soon come down from its perch and use the bath—and when the bottom is replaced the cage will be perfectly clean and dry. If you put the bath-tub in the cage, dry up all splashes of water after the bird has finished bathing.

5. *Of Food and Water.*—Simple diet is better for song birds than dainties, like cake, sugar and other "goodies." A mixture of rape and canary, with a *little* hemp seed (less of the latter in Summer than in Winter). If the bird is young the hemp seed should be cracked before using. In Summer the cage should be supplied with green food, such as cabbage, turnip tops, chick-weed, plantain stems, celery, water cress, etc. In Winter use a little sweet apple, and occasionally a trifle of boiled carrot or cauliflower, without salt. Birds also enjoy pieces of water cracker or pilot bread suspended in the cage, and particularly a cuttle fish bone, which is useful to them for the lime it contains. The seed box of the cage should be filled at night, for the bird's day is from sunrise to sunset and he wants to breakfast early, before you are up in the morning. Always see that the water cup is well filled. Birds frequently suffer intolerably from thirst after having scattered and wasted the water.

6. *Of Breeding Canaries.*—Breeding cages should be of polished wood, with one end and one side of wire. The floors should be coved with oil-cloth or stiff paper which can be removed, cleansed and re-sanded as required. A small box for nests so fastened that you can take it out at

will should be placed near the wooden corner of the cage about half way up; and material for nests, such as soft moss, wool, feathers, new cotton or hair, should be attached loosely to the wires where the bird can get them. Canaries pair about the middle of March or April. Select a vigorous, handsome pair, and having first kept them in separate cages within sight of each other for a few days, put them in the cage. Place the cage in a light, airy room with even temperature, and out of the draughts of cold air. In case the hen bird forsakes her nest after having laid her full nest of eggs and begun to set on them, remove the nest and put in a fresh one and let her take a new start. Canaries usually lay from four to six eggs, and they set for thirteen days. While the bird is setting she should have plenty of food; and on the day the hatching is expected, put into the cage, a little grated bread soaked in water and pressed dry, and part of a finely chopped hard-boiled egg should also be put in the cage. These viands are for the young birds. They should be placed in the cage at night or early in the morning, and great care should be taken to change them often enough so that they will not get sour. Healthy young birds will look red, and their crops will be full. If they seem pale and emaciated, it is time to suspect vermin, and you should change the nest at once, smoothing out the new one before putting the infants into it by rolling a hot hen's egg about in it. When twelve days old the young canaries begin to get feathers of their own and help themselves; and when they are a month old they may be taken from the parent cage to another near at hand and within sight. Their cage should never be without green food. Fresh hard-boiled eggs and grated bread, dipped in water and pressed, is the best food for them. Give them a chance to bathe daily; sprinkle them gently with water from a brush if they refuse to get into the tub; and let them have as much soft (not too hot) sunshine as possible. When in the sun there should always be a shady nook in the cage—a leafy branch or two, making a trembling shadow, is the best. If possible, let them have plenty of green food, and some insects, ants' eggs, &c. When the young birds are two weeks old, their parents often begin to get ready to prepare for the next brood; and if indications of such a state of things are seen. a new nest box and materials should be put in the breeding cage. The male will take care of the young birds while the mother busies herself with preparations for an increase of family.

A Suggestion.

To grate a nutmeg always commence at the blow end, and it will be solid clear through; while if you commence at the stem end, you will always find it hollow.

Try It.

Always set cake in a warm place by the stove for a few minutes after taking it from the oven.

Rich cheese feels soft under the pressure of the finger.

Keep yeast in wood or glass.

Keep preserves and jellies in glass.

Keep salt in a dry place.

Keep meal and flour in a cool dry place.

Keep vinegar in wood or glass.

Lard for pastry should be used hard as it can be cut with a knife. It should be cut through the flour, not rubbed.

Keep fresh lard in tin vessels.

Kettles are cleansed of onion and other odors, by dissolving a teaspoon of soda in the water used in washing them.

Wall paper may be cleaned by using fine dry Indian meal, rubbing it on with a soft dry cloth.

Recipe or Receipt: both words are correct.

Drink a goblet of rich milk every night before retiring.

Papering and painting are best done in cold weather, especially the latter, for the wood absorbs the oil of paint much more in warm weather; while in cold weather the oil hardens on the outside, making a coat which will protect the wood instead of soaking into it.

Never paper a wall over old paper and paste. Always scrape down thoroughly. Old paper can be got off by dampening with saleratus and water. Then go over all the cracks of the wall with plaster of Paris, and finally put on a wash of a weak solution of carbolic acid. The best paste is made out of rye flour, with two ounces of glue dissolved in each quart of paste; half an ounce of powdered borax improves the mixture.

Old boot-top linings make excellent iron-holders.

A hot shovel held over varnished furniture will take out white spots.

To Color Black.
Mrs. Mary King.

For one pound of cloth, take one oz. blue vitriol, dissolve in a kettle of soft water, then put in goods and boil them one hour; take out goods and add one oz. extract logwood, let it dissolve, then take from the fire and add one-half teaspoonful soda, return it to the stove and put in goods. Stir and turn until they become a good black. Wash in suds.

For Yellow.
Mrs. Mary King.

One-half pound sugar of lead, dissolve in hot water, one-quarter pound bichromate of potash dissolved in cold water in a wooden dish. Dip first in the solution of lead and then in the potash, until the color is dark enough. This will color five pounds.

To Color Black.
Mrs. H. L. Hervey.

Before coloring boil your goods well for an hour in strong soap suds, rinse well to take out soap and color.

One and one-half oz. extract logwood, one oz. bichromate potash, one oz. glue, seven or eight drops oil vitriol. Make a dye of the logwood, put in half the glue, (dissolved in a pint of warm water) and the vitriol. Let it come to a boil, put in the goods, stir constantly for three-quarters of an hour (and boil all the time), take out, let it drain, make a dye of the potash, put in the rest of the glue, let it come to boiling heat; put in your goods a few minutes, (but not boil) take out, drain, hang up to dry without rinsing.

To Color Carpet Rags.
Mrs. Louisa Talcott.

Blue:—For one lb. of cloth. One oz. of prussiate of potash in eight quarts warm water, one tablespoonful of copperas in eight quarts warm water, one tablespoonful oil of vitriol in eight quarts *hot* water. Dip the goods first in the copperas water, then in the potash, and last in the vitriol, then hang up a short time to air. If not deep enough wet them over again in the same way. Rinse in cold water.

Green:—After coloring the goods blue, dip into a yellow dye and rinse.

Yellow:—For one pound cloth. Two oz. sugar of lead in eight quarts warm water, one oz bichromate potash in eight quarts warm water. Dip the goods first in the potash water, and then in the sugar of lead.

For Orange.
Mrs. M. King.

Slack stone lime with boiling water and let it settle; drain it off and bring it to a scalding heat, and dip in your yellow. Dip but a few pieces at a time, and then get a new supply of lime water.

For Blue.
Mrs. M. King.

Two ounces Prussian or Chinese blue, one ounce oxalic acid; dissolve them together in a glass can; pour on water enough to wet the goods; this will color two pounds. They do not need to boil at all.

For Green.
Mrs. M. King.

Dip the dyed blue goods in a solution of sugar of lead (the same strength as for coloring yellow), then in the solution of bichromate of potash.

For Cochineal Red.
Mrs. M. King.

To one pound woolen goods infuse into water one ounce of cream tartar; stir it well; when the heat has increased a little, add one ounce pounded cochineal; mix well immediately; then add two ounces muriate of tin; stir it well; when it boils, put in the goods, wet; move briskly a few times, then more slowly. Let it boil twenty minutes, rinse in cold water, and dry in the shade.

Light Silver Drab.
Mrs. M. King.

For five pounds of goods one small teaspoon alum, and extract logwood about the same amount; boil well together, then dip the goods an hour. If not dark enough, add equal quantities of logwood and alum until suited.

Dark Snuff-brown for Woolen Goods.
Mrs. M. King.

For five pounds of goods, one pound camwood; boil fifteen minutes, and dip the goods three-quarters of an hour. Take out the goods and add two and one-half pounds fustic to the dye; boil ten minutes and dip the goods three-quarters of an hour, then add one ounce blue vitriol and four ounces copperas; dip again one-half hour; if not dark enough, add more copperas. It is dark and permanent.

The Teeth and Their Care.
J. H. SeCheverell.

No portion of our physical structure is of greater importance than the teeth, and it is also true, that, in the majority of cases, less attention is given them than is devoted to the thousand and one trivials of outside adornment. In their care the first thing to be considered is cleanliness. The mouth should be thoroughly cleansed after each meal. Parents, impress this fact upon the minds of your children early in life. In many mouths simply brushing the teeth with water will suffice; in others, a dentifice will be required to keep the teeth white. This need not be expensive. The following, which can be obtained at any druggist's, at a cost of a few cents, will be found fully equal to the extensive advertised, high priced tooth preparations:

R̥   Creta preparata   2 oz.
       Arris root, pulverized 2 oz.

M — Scent with a few drops of cinnamon, wintergreen, or any essential oil you prefer. Apply by moistening the finger, dipping in the powder and rubbing briskly across the teeth, following with brush and water.

In the selection of a brush be particularly careful to get one sufficiently soft, that it will not induce bleeding of the gums; and, in its use, not only pass it across the outer surface of the teeth, but between them and inside as well. Many pass floss silk between the teeth to dislodge any particles of food that may have lodged there. Many also use charcoal, pomice stone and other gritty substances as a tooth powder. *Don't do it*, unless you desire to destroy your teeth in the most speedy manner possible. A safe rule is, not to use anything on the teeth unless upon the advice of a competent dentist.

Parents, pay close attention to your children's teeth during the period of second dentition; and it is well at this time to have them examimed by your dentist, at least two or three times each year. You will thus, in may cases, avoid those irregularities of the teeth so annoying, especially to females, in after life.

Too little attention is paid to caries in the children's teeth. Some stormy night the little one comes in, perchance with wet feet, and one aching tooth. A night of agony follows; hot ashes, hops, liniment, camphor, laudanum, and whatever else comes handy, is brought into requisition to ease the pain. Finally morning dawns, and the poor little, worn-out sufferer is hurried away to the dentist, or more frequently, the family physician, and forced to endure the torture of an extraction, it may be, to the serious detriment of the germ of the permanent tooth. A little forethought on the part of the parents would have prevented all this. Your dentist could have applied a temporary filling to the tooth, which, if honestly done, would have preserved the tooth until such time as nature should displace it to make room for the second or permanent one. If you will persist in allowing their teeth to decay, for their sake, get a vial of the following, which, if applied to the tooth on a little cotton, will instantly relieve the pain:

℞   Chloroform, ½ oz.
   Aconite, ½ oz.

M — Label poison, and keep in secure place until needed. Follow the fore-going simple advice, that your children may, in after years,

"Rise up and call you blessed."

Tooth Wash.

The safest, cheapest, and most efficient, a piece of castile soap with brush every morning.

INDEX.

SOUPS.................................... 7
   Bean.................................... 8
   Beef..................................... 8
   Browning for Soups........... 8
   Celery................................. 9
   Chicken.............................. 9
   Fish Chowder, (1)............. 9
   " " (2)............. 9
   French Vegetable.............. 9
   Harvest.............................. 11
   Noodles.............................. 10
   Stock for Sup.................... 10
   Tomato............................... 10

SHELL FISH........................ 12
   Clam Chowder................. 16
   " Stew............................ 16
   Lobster Croquettes............ 12
   " Cutlets..................... 12
   " Rissoles................... 12
   Oysters broiled................... 12
   " fried, (1).................. 12
   " " (2).................. 13
   " Pie........................... 13
   " pickled..................... 13
   " with Toast................ 14
   " roasted................... 14
   " fancy roast.............. 14
   " stewed.................... 14
   " Maryland stewed..... 14
   " Yacht stew.............. 15
   " fritters.................... 15
   " panned.................. 15
   " scalloped................ 15
   " soup plain.............. 16
   " soup with milk........ 16

FISH...................................... 17
   Codfish, how to cook......... 17
   " on toast................ 17
   " balls..................... 18
   Fish fritters....................... 18
   " cakes.......................... 18
   " baked........................ 18
   " white, baked............. 18
   " fresh, " 19
   " flaked........................ 19

FISH.—*Continued*.
   Mackerel, salt. boiled......... 19
   " fresh 19
   Fish pie............................... 20
   " salad........................ 20
   Shad baked....................... 18
   Salmon pickled.................. 19

POULTRY............................. 21
   Chestnut stuffing............... 22
   Chicken pot-pie.................. 21
   " fried....................... 21
   " scalloped............... 22
   " good way to cook.. 22
   " Red Brook Mushroom fry............... 23
   " pie........................ 23
   " " crust............... 23
   " with oysters stewed 23
   " baked, (1).............. 24
   " " (2)............ 25
   " loaf....................... 24
   " pressed................ 24
   How to choose poultry........ 21
   Macaroni timbles................ 24
   Turkey, roast..................... 23
   " scalloped............... 22

MEATS................................. 26
   Beefsteak scalloped............ 27
   " broiled................. 27
   " baked.................. 27
   " with onions......... 27
   " " mushrooms.. 27
   Beef roast.......................... 28
   " loaf........................... 28
   " rechauffe................... 29
   " pounded.................... 29
   " heart......................... 30
   " liver.......................... 30
   " tongue boiled............ 30
   " deviled..................... 30
   " rissoles..................... 29
   " dried, in cream......... 30
   " frizzled..................... 30
   " with scrambled eggs... 30
   " omelet, or veal loaf..... 34
   " minced..................... 31

MEATS.—*Continued.*

Meat, frying 26
" prepared 28
" croquettes 29
" pie with potato crust.. 31
Meat, or chicken dumplings 31
Rissoles, or meat balls 29
Rules for boiling meats 26
Tongue, how to boil 30

MUTTON or LAMB 31
Lamb roast 31
" chops breaded 31
" cutlets a la Duchesse. 32
" steaks, how to fry 32
" spiced 32
" chops stewed 32
Mutton chops 32
" Irish stew 32
" ragout 33

VEAL 33
Sweetbreads fried 29
" 29
Veal spiced 33
" potted 33
" cutlets, (1) 33
"   "   (2) 33
" loaf 34
" scallop 34
" croquettes 34
" pie 34
" minced 34

PORK 36
Ham toast, (1) 36
"   "   (2) 36
" baked 36
Pork steaks 36
" and apples fried 36
Sausage, (1) 35
" (2) 35
" (3) 35
" (4) 35
" bologna 35
Scrapple 35
Spare ribs broiled 36

RELISHES FOR MEAT 37
Celery sauce 37
Cranberry " 27
Egg   " 37
Mint   " 37
Oyster   " 37
Tomato   " (1) 37
"   " (2) 37
"   " (3) 37

SALADS 38
Cabbage 39
Chicken, (1) 38
"   (2) 38
"   (3) 38
Dressing 38
Egg 39
Salmon 38
Salad dressing 39

GAME 40
Duck or Teal, roasted 41
Pigeon compote 41
Partridges, Pheasants, or
    Quails, roast 40
Pigeon pie 41
Pigeon roasted, (1) 41
"   "   (2) 41
Quail or Woodcock, boiled.. 41
Rabbit fried 41
"   stewed 41
Venison steak, broiled 40
"   to cook 40
Wild fowl roasted 40

VEGETABLES 42
Asparagus 45
Beans, lima 42
Beans, string 44
"   baked 44
"   with pork, baked 44
Cabbage baked 44
Cauliflower 46
Cheese straws 44
Corn oysters 43
"   fried 43
"   oyster cakes 43
Eggplant baked 45
"   fried 45
Macaroni as a vegetable 47
"   with cheese 45
"   stewed 47
"   with oysters 46
Mushrooms, French canned.. 46
Mushrooms, how to cook ... 46
"   broiled 46
Onion scalloped 45
Potatoes boiled 43
"   stewed 42
"   puff 43
"   Lyonnaise 42
"   Saratoga chips 43
Parsnips fried 46
"   fritters 46

INDEX.

VEGETABLES.—Continued.
Salsify 44
Spinach 46
Tomatoes baked 47
" broiled 47
" browned 47
" scalloped 47
Turnips 45

EGGS 48
Egg baskets 48
" sandwiches 49
" baked 48
" boiled 48
" fried 48
" parched 49
" scrambled 48
" stuffed 49
Omelet, (1) 49
" (2) 49

BREAD 50
Selecting flour 50
Bread, white 52
" salt rising 51
" brown, (1) 54
" " (2) 54
" Boston brown, (1) 54
" " " (2) 54
" corn, (1) 55
" " (2) 56
" Graham, (1) 54
" " (2) 54
" " (3) 54
" Indian, (1) 55
" " (2) 55
Biscuit raised 53
Johnny cake, (1) 55
" " (2) 55
Rolls, Parker house, (1) 52
" " " (2) 53
" French 52
Rusk 53
" sweet 53
Yeast 50
" hop 50
" dry hop, (1) 50
" " (2) 51
" railroad for salt rising. 51

BREAKFAST CAKES 56
Breakfast cakes 56
" corn cakes 57
" rolls 57
" cakes, oatmeal ... 57

BREAKFAST CAKES.-Continued.
Gems, graham, (1) 56
" " (2) 57
" wheat 57
Griddle cakes 57
Muffins, (1) 56
" (2) 56
" (3) 56
" wheat 56
" meal 56
Rice croquettes 57

CRACKERS 58
Crackers 58
" cream 58

CAKE 59
Cake making 59
Almond cake 65
Angel's food, (1) 71
" " (2) 71
Apple jelly 61
Bride's 72
Blackberry 65
Buffalo cream 67
Bridgeport 59
Cup 59
Coffee, (1) 69
" (2) 69
" (3) 70
Cream, (1) 68
" (2) 68
" puffs 68
Cocoanut, (1) 63
" (2) 63
Chocolate, (1) 63
" (2) 63
Cornstarch, (1) 72
" (2) 72
Carolina, (1) 74
" (2) 74
Charlotte Russe 84
Custard for cake, (1) 68
" " (2) 75
" ruse 75
Delicate 72
" plum 60
" fruit 60
Dover 60
Election 68
" "Old" 69
Fig, (1) 65
" (2) 65
French cream 67

INDEX.

CAKE.—*Continued.*

French loaf	69
Fruit, (1)	73
" (2)	73
" (3)	73
" cheap	73
" excellent	73
" black	73
" dark	73
" poor man's	73
" white	72
" delicate	62
Gold	60
Hickory-nut, (1)	65
" (2)	65
Ice cream	67
Jelly, (1)	60
" (2)	61
Layer, (1)	60
" (2)	63
Lemon jelly	61
" roll	61
Lemon	61
Loaf, (1)	69
" (2)	69
Marble, (1)	66
" (2)	66
Mottled	66
Metropolitan	66
Mountain, (1)	64
" (2)	64
" (3)	64
One egg	59
Ocean	60
Old Election	69
Orange, (1)	64
" (2)	64
" (3)	64
Plaid	74
Pork, (1)	70
" (2)	70
Raised	69
Ribbon	62
Rochester	60
Rolled jelly	60
Silver	72
Snowdrift	72
Spice, (1)	70
" (2)	70
" (3)	70
Sponge, (1)	61
" (2)	62
" (3)	62
" (4)	62

CAKE.—*Continued.*

Sponge, White, (1)	62
" " (2)	62
Snowflake	63
Vanity	75
Watermelon	67
White, (1)	71
" (2)	71
" (3)	71
" (4)	71
White-faced	72
White pound	59
ICINGS	76
Boiled, (1)	76
" (2)	76
" (3)	76
" (4)	76
For orange cake	76
COOKIES	77
Cookies, (1)	77
" (2)	77
" (3)	77
" (4)	77
" (5)	77
" (6)	77
" (7)	78
" (8)	78
Cream cookies	78
"Red Brook"	77
Seed cakes	78
Sugar drop	78
Water	78
Without eggs	78
GINGER COOKIES	79
Drop ginger cakes	79
Ginger drops	79
Ginger cakes	79
Graham cookies, (1)	79
" " (2)	79
Ginger snaps, (1)	80
" " (2)	80
" " (3)	80
" " (4)	80
Lemon snaps	80
Molasses cakes	79
Spiced ginger snaps	80
GINGER BREAD	81
Ginger bread, (1)	81
" " (2)	81
" " (3)	81
" " (4)	82

GINGER BREAD.—*Continued.*
  Card.. 82
  Cake.. 81
  Old fashioned, (1).................... 82
    "   "   (2)................... 82
  Pop overs..................................... 82
  Soft ginger bread, (1)............... 81
    "   "   "   (2).............. 81
    "   "   "   (3)............. 81
    "   "   "   (4)............. 82
  Water... 82

DOUGHNUTS................................... 83
  Doughnuts, (1)........................... 83
    "   (2)........................... 83
    "   (3)........................... 83
  Raised doughnuts..................... 83
  Fried cakes, (1).......................... 83
    "   "   (2)..................... 83
    "   "   (3)..................... 83
    "   "   (4)..................... 84
    "   "   (5)..................... 84
  Soda fried cakes without
    eggs... 84
  Quick fried cakes..................... 83

CRULLERS....................................... 85
  Crullers, (1)................................. 85
    "   (2)................................. 85
    "   (3)................................. 85
    "   fritters, (1).................. 85
    "   "   (2)................. 85

PIE CRUST....................................... 86
  Crust, (1)...................................... 86
    "   (2)...................................... 86
    "   (3)...................................... 86
  Graham crust............................. 86
  Glazed crust................................ 86
  Puff paste..................................... 86

PIES.. 91
  Almond tarts............................... 91
  Apple... 90
  Apple or peach Meringue..... 90
  Cream, (1)..................................... 88
    "   (2)..................................... 88
    "   (3)..................................... 88
  Cream Currant........................... 89
  Custard.. 89
  Dried peach................................. 90
  German.. 90
  Lemon, (1).................................... 87
    "   (2).................................... 87

PIES.—*Continued.*
  Lemon, (3)..................................... 87
    "   (4)..................................... 87
    "   (5)..................................... 87
    "   (6)..................................... 88
    "   (7)..................................... 88
  Lemon cream............................. 86
  Lemon custard.......................... 87
  Mince.. 89
  Mock mince................................ 90
  New England mince.............. 89
  Pumpkin, (1)............................... 90
    "   (2)............................... 90
  Rhubarb.. 91
  Shells for tarts........................... 91
  Silver... 91
  Summer mince.......................... 89

PUDDINGS...................................... 97
  Apple... 97
    "   dumpling........................ 92
    "   short cake..................... 93
  Baked blackberry.....................100
  Baked Indian, (1)..................... 96
    "   "   (2)..................... 96
  Batter... 96
  Bird's nest................................... 99
  Black.. 98
  Bread.. 99
  Cake.. 99
  Congress....................................... 92
  Cornstarch.................................. 98
  Cottage, (1).................................. 92
    "   (2).................................. 92
  English... 94
  English plum.............................. 94
  Fig.. 94
  Ginger.. 96
  Lemon.. 95
  Lemon rice................................... 93
  Old-fashioned Indian............ 96
  Orange... 98
  Paste, (1)....................................... 97
    "   (2)....................................... 97
  Peach tapioca............................. 96
  Rice, (1)... 93
    "   (2)... 94
  Rich suet...................................... 98
  Roly poly...................................... 97
  Snow... 97
  Sour cream................................. 97
  Southern rice............................. 93
  Spanish cream.......................... 97
  Steamboat................................... 97

INDEX.

PUDDINGS.—*Continued.*
Steamed, (1)...... 94
" (2)...... 95
" (3)...... 95
Steamed blackberry 95
Suet, (1)...... 98
" (2)...... 99
" (3)...... 99
" (4)...... 99
Tapioca, (1)...... 95
" (2)...... 95
" (3)...... 95
Tapioca and apple 96
Whortleberry 100

PUDDING SAUCE......101
Foam, (1)......102
" (2)......102
" (3)......102
Hard sauce......101
Sauce, (1)......101
" (2)......101
" (3)......101
" (4)......101
" (5)......102
Sauce for ginger pudding....101

AMBROSIA, CUSTARDS, &c...103
A delicate dessert......107
Ambrosia, (1)......103
" (2)......103
Angel's food......103
Apple cream......106
" snow......104
Blanc Mange......104
Boiling rice......103
Charlotte Russe, (1)......105
" " (2)......105
Cronstades......104
Custard......104
Floating Island......103
Friar's Omelet......107
Fried cream......105
Iced apple......105
Ice cream......107
Imitation cream......107
Lemon ice......107
Rice custard......106
Strawberry Frapees......108
Tapioca cream, (1)......105
" " (2)......106
" " (3)......106

PICKLES......109
Brine for pickles......109
Cauliflower......114
Chili Sauce, (1)......115
" " (2)......115
Chopped pickles, (1)......112
" " (2)......112
Chow-Chow, (1)......112
" (2)......112
Cold Slaw, dressing for......114
Cucumbers, (1)......109
" (2)......110
Cucumbers, to put down for Winter......109
French......111
Green color in pickles......109
Hot Slaw......114
Melon rind......114
Mixed pickles......111
Mushroom......115
Onion, (1)......113
" (2)......113
Peaches......114
Pickalilli, (1)......113
" (2)......113
Pickles......110
Ripe cucumbers, (1)......110
" " (2)......110
Spanish......111
Spiced fruit......115
" grapes, (1)......115
" " (2)......115
" citron......116
" plums......116
Tomatoes, (1)......111
" (2)......111
Tomato catsup......114
" chowder......113
" relish......113

FRUITS, JELLIES, PRESERVES, &c......117
Apples baked, old-fashioned, 119
Apple compote......119
" jelly......118
" " old-fashioned......119
Apples spiced......123
Citron preserves......121
Cranberries, how to cook....119
Fruit jelly, how to make......117
Grape jam......120
" jelly......119
Gooseberry jam......123
Green sweetmeats......121

160 INDEX.

FRUITS, &c.—Continued.
Lemon jelly, (1) 118
" " (2) 118
Peaches to preserve 122
Plum, wild, to preserve 120
Quince Marmalade 122
" Souffle 122
" to preserve 121

CONFECTIONERY 124
Carmels 124
Chocolate carmels, (1) 124
" " (2) 124
Cocoanut candy 125
Cream candy 124
Marbled cream candy 124
Molasses taffy 124
Nut candy 125
Taffy 125

DRINKS 126
Chocolate 126
Coffee, (1) 126
" (2) 126
Prepared cocoa 126
Substitute for cream 126

FOR THE SICK ROOM 127
Apple water 129
Arrow root custard 130
Baked milk 132
Beef tea, (1) 127
" " (2) 128
" " and rice 133
Blackberry wine 131
Calves foot jelly 127
Chicken jelly 130
Corn meal gruel 128
Cough syrup 131
Cracked wheat 130
Cream soup 130
Croup 132
Cup pudding 129
Cure for chilblains 134
Disinfectant, (1) 133
" (2) 133
Dried flour 128
Drink for the sickroom 129
Dysentery 133
Dyspepsia 132
Earache 134
Egg gruel 142
Fits 133
Ginger beer 131

FOR THE SICK ROOM.—Contin'd.
Graham hasty puddings 127
Hoarseness 132
Hop bitters 135
Indian meal gruel 127
inflammation salve 134
Jellice 129
Milk porridge, (1) 127
" " (2) 130
Milk and rice gruel 131
Mountain custard 128
Mutton broth, (1) 127
" " (2) 128
Mrs. Garfield's beef extract, 128
Oatmeal gruel 129
Ointment for chapped hands,134
Panada 129
Poison antidotes 134
Raspberry shrub 132
Remedy for croup 132
Sago custard 132
Sago jelly pudding 130
Tapioca jelly 129
Thickened milk 131
Toothache drops, (magic)... 133
To remove grease from broths 132
To stop flow of blood 134
Wash for the hair 135
Wash for the sickroom 130
White balsam salve 134
Wine Whey 131

MISCELLANEOUS 136
Ammonia, different uses of.. 145
Acid stains, to remove 144
Ants, to drive away 141
Beef brine 136
Birds—culture and care of canaries 146
Bleaching solution 138
Bleaching cloth 138
Blueing, cheap 138
Boths, to clean 140
Brass, to clean 142
Black dresses, to clean 144
Burns, cure for 137
Cologne water 137
Cement for broken china,(1) 141
" " " (2) 141
Crape, to clean 141
Coloring 150
Certain suggestions 149
Decanters, to clean 140

MISCELLANEOUS.—Continued.

Eggs, preserving, (1) 136
" " (2)............136
Feathers, to clean..............144
" to kill moths in ...140
Faded garments, to renovate, 144
Grease spots, to remove......144
Glass, to cut.....................139
Glass stoppers, to remove...139
Hair-brushes, to clean..........139
Hams, to cure 136
Ink, indelible 137
Ink-stains, to remove..........140
" " from books, 141
Iron-rust, to remove...........142
Mucilage..........................139
Mosquitoes, to drive away...141
Mildew, from linen to remove................................143
Plumes, curling..................145
Pillows, airing...................140
Putty, to remove................139
Potatoes, to prevent from shriveling. 139
Rats, to expel....................141

MISCELLANEOUS.—Continued.

Removing white stains from dark wood....................142
Soap, shaving....................137
Starch polish 137
Silk, dressing....................144
To sour vinegar quickly.......136
To wash clothes without fading 138
To wash doubtful calicoes...138
To set colors in calicoes and stockings..........................138
To remove stains from clothing 140
To remove stains from white goods.................... 143
To mend china..................141
Tinware, to clean 142
Table for housewives 139
Traveling lunch.................140
The bird fancier................146
The teeth and their care.....152
Washing fluid....................137
Worms and slugs, to kill 141
Wine stains on marble........142

www.ingramcontent.com/pod-product-compliance
Lightning Source LLC
Chambersburg PA
CBHW030257170426
43202CB00009B/783